Cen
NT
17.95

MONET

His Life and Complete Works

SOPHIE MONNERET

In Collaboration With
AGNÈS LIEBAERT

LONGMEADOW
PRESS

ISBN: 0-681-10474-0

Printed in Spain by
Fournier Artes Gráficas, S.A.

Editor:

Clotilde de Bellegarde

Designer:

Luis F. Balaguer

Editorial Assistants:

José Antonio Vázquez

Patricia Núñez Millieri

Rosa Vallribera i Fius

Albert Pujol Gámiz

English Translation:

Richard Jacques / Discobole

Design Assistants:

Manuel Domingo Pérez

Miguel Ortíz Català

Publishing Assistant:

Monserrat Juan Peña

Contents

Claude Manet

Born in Paris in 1840, Claude-Oscar Monet spent his childhood in Le Havre where his parents, Adolphe and Louise-Justine Monet, moved in 1845 with his elder brother Léon, born in 1836. His father went to the port when it was at the height of its industrial transformation on the advice of his half-sister, Marie-Jeanne Lecadre. From then on, Adolphe Monet worked in his brother-in-law's wholesale grocery business. Ships docking alongside the quay, sails disappearing over the horizon; the sea was already imprinted on the painter's first childhood "impressions."

At school his teacher François Ochard, a former pupil of David, was aware of his gifts for art, and young Monet, a great admirer of Daumier, became famous for his caricatures of leading figures of the town. Signed Oscar Monet and sold at a louis each, they were exhibited at the shop of a stationer and engraver, Gravier. Thanks to him, Monet was introduced to the landscape painter Eugène Boudin, who took him under his wing and took him out to paint in the open air. A fruitful meeting. "If I became a painter, I owe it to Boudin," said Monet later. On the death of his mother in 1857, his aunt Marie-Jeanne Lecadre, a talented amateur painter who moved in artistic circles, took care of his education. In 1858 the Le Havre exhibition hung his first picture, *A View of Rouelles*, which showed the influence of the school of 1830 (Dupré, Chintreuil, Daubigny); in his sketchbooks landscapes alternated with comic caricatures. His success as a caricaturist, his aunt's contacts, and his own fierce will persuaded his father to let him take up a career as an artist, on one condition however: that he enroll at the École des Beaux-Arts in Paris to receive a high quality training. His first application for a grant was turned down, but Monet had not waited for the reply. He was already in Paris, where at the age of 18, he discovered the charms and vicissitudes of the life of an art student: visits to senior painters; to Troyon, a friend of Boudin; to Amand Gautier, a relative of his aunt Lecadre and a disciple of Courbet; hours spent in front of the masters in the Louvre; enrollment at the Académie Suisse, where he met Pissarro. Young Monet spent a good deal of his time at the Brasserie des Martyrs, the stronghold of Realism where he caught a glimpse of Courbet, the critic Castagnary, and the budding novelist Alphonse Daudet. In the Latin Quarter he ran into Clemenceau,

Engraving of Le Havre, the city where Monet spent his childhood and adolescence. At that time the port of Le Havre was already one of the most important in France.

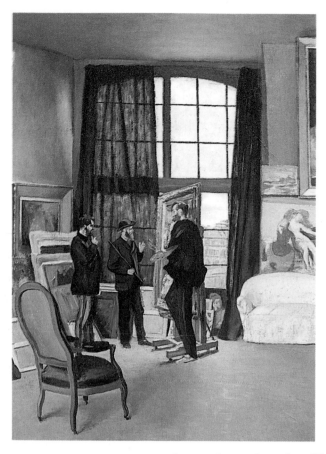

Bazille, detail of The Artist's Studio, Rue La Condamine *(Musée d'Orsay, Paris). The new generation of painters were moving away from the realism of Courbet to follow Manet. Bazille shared his studio with young painters such as Renoir and Monet.*

a medical student in those days; years later he would become a loyal friend.

At the Salon of 1859 Monet particularly admired Daubigny, but also the Orientalists, an interest which may have been at the root of his choice of the First regiment of the Chasseurs d'Afrique when the luck of the draw forced him to do his military service. In June 1861 he left for Algeria in search of the Orient of the painters. But after a year his service was interrupted by an attack of typhoid fever. "The impressions of light and color I received there were only classified later, but the seed of my future investigations had been planted," he said in an interview in 1900.

On his return to Le Havre he had another decisive meeting on the beach at Sainte-Adresse with the Dutch landscape painter Jongkind, of whom he said: "From that moment on he was my master and it is to him that I owe the final education of my eye." Monet returned to his life in Paris under the aegis of his cousin by marriage, the society painter Auguste Toulmouche, who had been entrusted with the task of restricting his expenses and supervising his studies. Thanks to his recommendation, in the autumn of 1862 he registered at the Gleyre studio, where students from different countries followed the liberal teaching of the Swiss painter. There he met what was to be the battalion of Impressionism: Renoir, Bazille, and Sisley. From time to time the group made their escape from Paris to paint from life: at Chailly-en-Bierre (near Barbizon), which Monet discovered with Bazille in 1863; at Le Havre and Honfleur, where Mère Toutain lodged the most passionate marine painters at the Saint-Siméon farm. His friends Jongkind and Boudin were among the number and passed on to him the example of their airy, unselfconscious style. The year 1864 yielded a harvest of studies, both freer and more solid: *The Lieutenancy at Honfleur, The Hospice Lighthouse, The Pointe de la Hève.* It was also the time of debt and the endless litany of requests for money, mostly from Bazille, the son a rich Protestant family from Montpellier, who shared his studio in the Rue Furstenberg with him. A canvas by their friend Gilbert de Sèverac depicts young Monet at that moment, when his career was about to take a decisive turn.

He had his first Salon and first success in 1865 with *The Mouth of the Seine at Honfleur*, which caught the eye of Paul Mantz, the critic for the *Gazette des Beaux-Arts*. Encouraged by that foretaste of fame, Monet began work on a vast, remarkably modern composition at Chailly: *The Picnic*, which he unfortunately failed to finish for the Salon of 1866. But he did enjoy his first triumph there with *Camille* or *The Green Dress*, a portrait of a young girl who had just entered his life, which he finished in eight days. In his first article on the Salon Zola bestowed some words of praise on him, while others commented ironically on the similarity of the names Monet and Manet. The all-powerful director of *L'Artiste*, Arsène Houssaye, bought the painting.

After that, Claude Monet existed; the critics could no longer ignore him. At the time he was, with Renoir, Bazille's guest at his new studio in the Rue Visconti. He spent the summer near Ville-d'Avray, where he painted the dazzling *Women in the Garden*; Courbet came to watch him at work.

He then returned to Honfleur and during the winter of 1866-1867 he painted his first snowy landscapes with several versions of *The Road to the Saint-Siméon Farm*. There was a disappointment in store for him in the spring; his works were turned down by the Salon because of the technique, which was considered too brutal by the members of the jury. Like Renoir, Monet then tackled subjects which had a good chance of finding a buyer that year of the Universal Exhibition: views of Paris. *Saint-Germain-l'Auxerrois*, *The Jardin de l'infante*, *The Quai du Louvre*, painted with isometric proportion, demonstrated his qualities as a painter of city landscapes.

At the time he was travelling backwards and forwards between the capital, where Camille was expecting a baby, and Sainte-Adresse, where his family had refused to hear of the liaison, but spoiled him outrageously. Guillemet, Guerbois' good-natured friend, was also working at Sainte-Adresse, and Sisley was at Honfleur. "I have twenty or so canvases which are well under way, some astonishing seascapes and figures and gardens, something of everything, in fact," he wrote to Bazille on 25 July 1867. On 8 August his first son, Jean, was born and he asked Bazille to be his godfather; the godmother was Julie Vellay, Pissarro's companion.

Ships leaving the Docks of Le Havre was much commented on at the Salon in 1868. Zola stressed the painter's modernity and originality in

Photograph of the church of Saint-Germain-l'Auxerrois seen from the Louvre. Monet painted the church from the windows of the museum. He was influenced by the topographical photographs of the day.

Boat trips in the outskirts of Paris were one of the most fashionable pastimes in the eighteen-seventies. Renoir and Monet set up their easels on the banks of the Seine and tirelessly painted the boats and boaters. The people in the boats were one of Monet's favorite themes and he devoted a series of six large canvases to them between 1887 and 1889.

a prophetic article: "I do not feel worried about him, he will tame the crowd when he wants."

The picture was accepted thanks to the support of Daubigny. Shortly afterwards, Monet spent some time at a hamlet on the banks of the Seine, Gloton; which Guillemet, who introduced him to Cézanne and Zola, must have recommended to him. There he painted a picture which foreshadowed the direction his style was soon to take, *Bennecourt*, the name of the village which can be seen on the opposite bank where Daubigny often dropped anchor with his floating studio accompanied by Corot and Guillemet.

Slipping away from Gloton he returned to Le Havre, where the International Maritime Exhibition, to which he had sent five canvases, was being held. Courbet, who was in town for the same event, took him to lunch with Alexandre Dumas at Étretat, which was probably what later encouraged him to come back and work there. *Ships leaving...* was bought at the exhibition by a member of the Saint-Siméon family, Louis-Joaquim Gaudibert, the son-in-law of a rich notary from Le Havre. The painter's first patron commissioned portraits from him – Monet did a masterly one of his wife: *Madame Gaudibert* – but most importantly he gave him an income which allowed him to settle with Camille and Jean at Étretat. He worked enthusiastically, his sole concern being that someone might get hold of the canvases he had left in Paris with Bazille. He did not miss the gatherings at the Café Guerbois, the headquarters of the discussions of the avant-garde around Manet, Degas, and Pissarro. "Everyone is too concerned with what they see and hear in Paris, however strong they may be, and what I do here at least has the merit of not being like what someone else is doing. At least, I think so."

That difference was clearly the cause of a new failure at the Salon in 1869. Monet drew consolation from an exhibition at the gallery of the art dealer Latouche, where one of the views of Sainte-Adresse, probably the superb *Terrace*, "aroused wild enthusiasm among the young people," as Boudin wrote at the time. Shortly after, he left Paris for Saint-Michel, a hamlet near Bougival which was the base camp for the whole Batignolles group that year. Sisley was at La Celle-Saint-Cloud, Pissarro at Louveciennes, near Renoir's parents. Renoir often joined Monet, and they shared a frugal life which led them to appeal on more than one occasion to the generosity of Bazille: "For eight days no wine, no fire in the kitchen, no light." That did not prevent them from going to work on the Île de Croissy, where they invented an aesthetic that marked a total break with the art of the day in their paintings of *La Grenouillère*. It was on account of a view of that fashionable pleasure garden that Monet was once again turned down at the Salon in 1870. To express his indignation, Daubigny, who had been supporting him for several years, resigned from the jury, and Corot left with him. On 28 June, just as rumors of war were becoming more ominous, Monet married Camille – Courbet was one of the witnesses – and left for Trouville, the most elegant of watering places, to paint beach scenes. As in previous summers, his friend Bazille was in Languedoc. He was never to see him again; Bazille was shot down by Prussian bullets in November.

After the first disasters of the Franco-Prussian War, the Republic, so dear to the Batignolles group, was proclaimed. The fighting went on, however, but Monet did not have to undergo the frightful siege of Paris or the dramas of the Commune which ruined his friend Courbet and drove him into exile. He joined the flood of refugees who left France as the enemy troops advanced and settled in London. There he found Pissarro and Daubigny, who introduced him to Durand-Ruel, a crucial encounter, as the great French art dealer began to show his works in his gallery in London and had them hung at the International Exhibition that was held in the city in the spring of 1871. Moreover, his contemplation of Turner's watercolors at the Victoria and Albert Museum exercized a certain influence on his manner of conceiving landscape; he managed to integrate their inventive freedom into his later work. He returned to France in the autumn of 1871 via Holland, which he knew through Jongkind. He was charmed by the windmills and canals of Zaandam. At the same time he started a collection of the Japanese prints so admired by Degas, Bracquemond, and Burty and whose style, as he had seen in London, had been assimilated by Whistler.

Japanese print by Chobunsai Yeishi (Museum of Oriental Art, Genoa). Monet felt a deep admiration for Japanese art, and like his contemporaries, including Degas, Gauguin, and Van Gogh, he drew inspiration from the prints he collected.

ARGENTEUIL

From that time the stages of his career bear the names of the villages where he chose to live because they were close to the water, an element which became more and more of an inspiration in his work. In 1871 he settled at Argenteuil (11 kilometers from Paris by train from the Gare de Saint-

10

Old photograph of Argenteuil. This small town near Paris provided Monet with everything he needed to work: peace and quiet and subject matter. The garden of his house and the banks of Seine were an endless source of inspiration for the artist.

Lazare), living successively in two houses until 1878. The first belonged to some friends of Manet and had been the home of Théodule Ribot. The housewarming (late 1871), to which Boudin came, was an artistic occasion. Moreover, his friends came there on the slightest pretext: Sisley, Manet – who was always a source of succor in times of distress – and Renoir, on whom fortune was beginning to smile. The beautiful Camille posed for the two of them and they became neighbors. In 1874 Manet painted *The Monet Family in the Garden*, while Renoir made a study for *Madame Monet and her Son on the Hill* two years after painting a portrait of their host reading and smoking a pipe. During the happy Argenteuil period the masterpieces began to accumulate. At the bottom of the garden, the Seine with its sailboats, rowing boats and barges provided an inexhaustible source of subjects. Following the example of Daubigny, Monet had a floating studio built, which allowed him to paint some unusual views of some of his favorite subjects: railway or road bridges. His brush immortalized the changing springtime of the Île-de-France, peopled by the fleeting silhouettes of Camille and Jean. Monet tirelessly painted the lilacs or the dahlias in his garden, the apple blossoms, and the meadows studded with poppies near the Argenteuil basin or the windmills of Sannois.

That fertile output did not pass unnoticed by Durand-Ruel, who bought 29 pictures in 1872. But there were new customers too, the bankers Albert and Henri Hecht, the critic Théodore Duret.

During a trip to Normandy in 1873, Monet painted views of Le Havre, Étretat, Sainte-Adresse, and undoubtedly, the famous *Impression, Sunrise*, incorrectly dated 1872.

At the same time, with Renoir, Pissarro, Degas, and Sisley, he took an active part in the foundation of a collective company which was a regrouping of the New School. Tired of the pronouncements of the Salon, the Batignolles group wanted to organize their own exhibition. That was accomplished in January 1874 with the birth of the cooperative limited company of painters, sculptors, and engravers, which had thirty members. An exchange of letters between Paul Alexis and Monet announced the event in the press. It only remained to find a venue. The photographer Nadar, an enthusiastic follower of the group, generously offered his premises in the Boulevard des Capucines. On 15 April, their first exhibition opened for one month. In the catalogue, there were 165 works signed by Boudin, Bracquemond, Cézanne, Degas, Guillaumin, Lépine, Berthe Morisot, Pissarro, Renoir, Sisley. Among the ones by Monet was a seascape destined for glory: *Impression, Sunrise*, whose author explained its genesis in these words: "I had sent something I had done at Le Havre, sun in the mist and the masts of a few ships sticking up... I was asked for a title for the catalogue. I answered: 'Put impression'." Louis Leroy responded by entitling his article in *Le Charivari*: "The Impressionists' Exhibition." The new school had found its name. A few months later the company was dissolved and the results of the collective sale organized in March 1875 at Drouot were disappointing.

In the meantime, Monet must have moved, though not far from his previous house.

The second Impressionist exhibition opened in 1876 at Durand-Ruel's gallery. Most of the views of Argenteuil hung by Monet belonged to a new enthusiast, the famous opera singer Jean-Baptiste Faure. Albert Wolff, the redoubtable critic of *Le Figaro*, lashed out at the exhibition of "alienated men, crazed by ambition." Once again Zola supported them with words of praise, but in a magazine sold in Russia.

As was his custom, Monet lived beyond his means, and hounded by his creditors, was often pressuring dealers and collectors, even at the risk of irritating some of his friends, such as Pissarro. But his hard work and talent brought him new customers: Rouart, Chocquet, the painter Caillebotte – who, in 1876, exhibited for the first time with the Impressionists – the publisher Georges Charpentier, Doctor de Bellio, and most important Ernest Hoschedé. This fabric merchant, a passionate lover of painting and married to the daughter of a wealthy Belgian metal founder, had bought *Impression, Sunrise* in 1874.

In 1876, Hoschedé commissioned Monet to paint four decorative panels for his Château de Rottenbourg in Montgeron. Working on the spot, Monet also did portraits of his hosts' family and several landscapes. One of them, *The Lake*, foreshadows *The Water Lilies*. Camille remained in Argenteuil, and the painter became involved with Alice Hoschedé, whose husband was often away on business.

On his return early in 1877, Monet rented a studio in the Rue Moncey, in the Europe district, and returned to painting urban subjects. He did

Photograph of Claude Monet taken by Benque. The artist was the object of savage criticism in the press and his economic situation was increasingly precarious. In 1879 he wrote to his friend Murer: "I am absolutely disgusted and discouraged with this existence of mine. When you get to this state at my age, there is nothing left to hope for."

some interiors and exteriors of the Gare Saint-Lazare, that landmark of the Paris of Haussmann. Overhead views, effects of perspective, mists; reinterpreting Impressionist technique he took it to its highest level. Sometimes the memory of Turner hovers over some of the canvases, such as *Tracks out of the Gare Saint-Lazare*. That modern style delighted Zola, who twelve years later in *The Beast in Man*, raised the locomotive to the rank of hero.

The landscapes were now inspired by the green spaces in the city. At the time of third Impressionist exhibition in 1877, Monet presented, apart from eight versions of the Gare Saint-Lazare – the beginning of a series for which he always retained a great affection – views of the Parc Monceau, the Île de la Grande-Jatte, and the Tuileries (done from Chocquet's apartment). At the exhibition the portrait of *Camille with Bouquet of Violets*, so modern in its construction, reveals the model in a sad state of weariness. At the house in Argenteuil the debts piled up. They could no longer count on Hoschedé, who was on the verge of ruin. Monet sent out numerous calls for help. To everyone, friends and collectors: Murer, Bellio, Gustave Manet, Charpentier. In January 1878 he had to pay off his debts and change houses again. Obliged to leave *The Picnic* as security to his landlord in Argenteuil, the painter returned to Paris, 26 Rue d'Édimbourg. There his second son, Michel, was born. Édouard Manet once again came to his rescue at a time of financial crisis.

On 30 June 1878 – the year of the Universal Exhibition – a festival of flags hung out in honor of the Republic transformed Paris into a dazzling palette of color. Monet transcribed it in his pre-Expressionist canvases: *The Rue Montorgueil, The Rue Saint-Denis*. It was by way of a farewell to urban subjects and the capital, where he was never to live again, though he kept a studio in the Rue de Vintimille where potential buyers could see his paintings.

VÉTHEUIL

After Argenteuil, Vétheuil, another of the prettiest sites on the banks of the Seine. He settled there in the summer of 1878 with his wife, their two children, and the Hoschedé family, now ruined, with their six children (Marthe, Blanche, Suzanne, Jacques, Germaine, and Jean-Pierre); not to mention a sizeable staff. The painter was delighted with the place; Vétheuil, its houses, its church, the meadows of Saint-Martin-la-Garenne appear in his canvases in the changing seasons. But the health of Camille, who had not gotten over the birth of her second son, deteriorated rapidly. She died on 5 September 1879 after prolonged suffering and Monet, as a final tribute, painted her features on her death bed. He did not even turn up for the fourth Impressionist exhibition, though, urged by Caillebotte. He sent twenty-nine landscapes "which look as if they were done in an afternoon," pontificated Wolff, while Burty proclaimed him "the most gifted artist of his generation."

Hoschedé had gone back to Paris to take care of his tottering business and Monet was left alone, unprotected, with Alice and the children, dogged by his creditors, but always slaving away at his work. The modifications to landscapes caused by variations in the weather had long been one of his major concerns. The bitter winter of 1879-1880, with its monumental freeze followed by a no less spectacular thaw, inspired effects of snow, of frost, of ice floes drifting on the water.

He had always been mad about gardening and transformed the steps

which led down to the Seine into a forest of sunflowers which inspired one of his most beautiful canvases, the *Steps at Vétheuil*, in which his joy of living seems to be reborn. He had two boats on the Seine below his house which allowed him to find the best vantage points for painting Vétheuil and Lavacourt, the village on the far bank.

Renoir's success at the Salon in 1879 encouraged Monet to follow his example. He was accepted at the 1880 number with a fairly classical view of *Lavacourt*, but he was called a quitter by his former friends (Degas, Pissarro) who persevered with the organization of exhibitions to which new members (Gauguin, Raffaelli) brought a different spirit. "The little church has now become a run-of-the-mill school which opens its door to the first person to come along," Monet declared to a journalist in *La Vie moderne* who had come to interview him at Vétheuil. His first one-man exhibition was held at the gallery of the same name which Georges Charpentier had just founded. Eighteen works were shown – views of Vétheuil and *The Ice Floes*, whose daring had scared the juries of the Salon. The preface to the catalogue was written by Théodore Duret who had published the first *Histoire des peintres impressionnistes* (History of the Impressionist Painters) in 1878, which had placed him at the head of the movement. Although Degas attacked the unbridled hullabaloo over the exhibition, at the age of forty Monet finally obtained some success with the critics. The American painter Sargent met him in 1876. Signac wrote to him: "I paint with just your works as a model, following the great path that you have pioneered for us." At that time Durand-Ruel began to buy regularly again and some new collectors appeared, some of them local,

Old photograph of Vétheuil. Monet did not understand artists who shut themselves up in a studio to paint. "...to draw, yes; to paint, no... Here is my studio," he said pointing to the little town of Vétheuil.

such as the Coquerets at Vétheuil, the composer Delius, Ratisbonne, or Deudon. His earlier seascapes had no trouble finding buyers, which encouraged him to make more trips to Normandy to the villa of his brother Léon at Petites-Dalles, near Fécamp.

Nevertheless, the painter's financial situation continued to deteriorate and the neighbors looked askance at the bizarre Monet-Hoschedé family. He had to move once again and find a place where the boys could go to school. Monet consulted Sisley about the advantages

Monet's house in Giverny. The painter wrote to his friend Mallarmé: "I am sorry to leave Giverny, all the more so now that I have fixed up the house and the garden to my taste."

of Moret-sur-Loing, then Zola about Poissy near Médan, where the novelist had moved in 1878. In spite of her husband's protests, Alice Hoschedé followed Monet to Poissy with her children in December 1881. But it was no more than an interlude. The painter did not find the same enchantment as at Argenteuil or Vétheuil and his output suffered in consequence. He seized every opportunity to escape from "horrible, wretched Poissy," where the house by the Seine was flooded at the slightest rise of the water. The coast of Normandy provided a refuge; in February and March 1882 he did a series of landscapes in Dieppe, Varengeville, and most of all, Pourville.

At the same time stormy quarrels and enmities were affecting the Impressionist group more strongly than ever. The collapse of the Banque Générale which backed Durand-Ruel had a devastating effect on him. In the face of a host of problems, he organized the seventh Impressionist exhibition in March 1882. Degas, who maintained his stance to the end, and Renoir refused to show with Gauguin, whom they considered too dictatorial. Berthe Morisot would accept only on condition that Monet give his agreement. Monet in turn would decide according to the attitude of Renoir and Caillebotte. In the end, Monet showed 30 pictures, of Vétheuil or Fécamp in Normandy, winter landscapes, views looking down from the top of cliffs, summer paths on the Île Saint-Martin. The critics were kind, the buyers encouraging.

During the summer in Pourville, Monet gave Blanche, the second of the Hosche-dé daughters, her first painting lesson. The portraits of *Madame Paul* and *Monsieur Paul* (Graff), restaurant owners and pastry cooks, which were done in exchange for cakes for the children, date from that visit.

Relations between Alice Hoschedé, who was used to a life with money, and Monet, permanently hounded by his creditors, were not without their difficulties, as their correspondence bears witness. Trivial incidents: "Remember that I love you and could not live without you," the painter wrote on 12 February 1883 from Étretat where he was working on some seascapes for Durand-Ruel. One of them, *Rough Sea at Étretat*, was painted in a storm which was so violent that he was obliged to take refuge in his room at the Hôtel Blanquet. The dealer who in 1882 had commissioned him to paint decorative panels for his drawing room devoted an exhibition to him in 1883. He presented 56 canvases, essentially paintings of Varengeville and Pourville. But it was a failure and Monet, most put out, reproached him with his lack of preparation for the show. The painter had been captivated by the new rooms at the Galerie Georges Petit, and unsuccessfully asked Durand-Ruel to come to an understanding with his colleague to exhibit the Impressionists on his premises.

Florian's engraving of a photograph of Monet taken by Robinson at Giverny. The painter and gardener wrote to Geffroy: "No, I am not a great painter or a great poet... I only know that I do what I can to express what I feel about nature."

GIVERNY

After Argenteuil, Vétheuil, and Poissy, it was now the turn of Giverny. At the age of 42, Monet found the haven to which he would return joyfully at the end of his painting campaigns. In April 1883 the Hoschedé and Monet families moved into a house with a large garden where the Epte flowed into the Seine. The happiness of the first days there was nevertheless clouded by the news of the death of Manet, the generous supporter of his youthful years, followed two years later by that of his brother Gustave. In December, feeling the need for renewed inspiration, Monet left with Renoir to discover the South, a journey which took them from Marseille to Genoa, with a stop at L'Estaque with Cézanne. Back in Paris for the Manet retrospective, he had only one idea: to return to the Riviera, but this time alone: "I ask you not to mention this journey to anyone... However pleasant it was to make the trip as a tourist with Renoir, it would be equally tiresome to make it in company to work," he confided to Durand-Ruel.

To Bordighera, then to Menton, Monet worked like a madman, doing fifty or so canvases with palm, orange, lemon, and olive trees in the garden of a certain Monsieur Moréno, "a true heaven on earth." He wrote to Alice that he was "working like a dog, going from one study to another, but thinking beatifically of Giverny in the evening. These palm trees will be my damnation."

He shared the works he did in the South between Portier, Petit, and Durand-Ruel, a proceeding which his loyal dealer, who had always been ready to support and encourage him since his early days, took as a betrayal. His reputation grew, his finances improved. In a letter to his wife, Gauguin wrote: "Monet is earning a hundred thousand francs a year now," a considerable sum at the time, when a student could live on a hundred and fifty francs a month.

The late summer of 1885 was spent in Étretat, one of his constant sources of inspiration. Faure placed his house at his disposal, and when Alice and the children left he moved back to the Hôtel Blanquet. He sometimes dined with Maupassant, that son of the Caux region, in a house he had at La Guillette. The novelist's descriptions and the painter's pictures evoke the same images: the Porte d'Amont and the Porte d'Aval, the spire, and the fleets of boats sailing out to sea.

Although he was settled at Giverny, Monet did not neglect the friendly or literary and artistic gatherings of Paris. Berthe Morisot and her husband, Manet, invited him with Renoir, Mallarmé, and Degas to their Thursday dinners; Mirbeau and Caillebotte accompanied him to the "Suburban dinners", presided over by Edmond de Goncourt. He also attended the "Good Cossacks dinners," where the painters Helleu, Renoir, and Cazin rubbed shoulders with the writers Mallarmé and Bergerat (director of *La Vie moderne*). Not forgetting the Impressionist dinners at the Café Riche. The talk was of painting, of course, but also of gardening with Caillebotte and Mirbeau, who were just as passionate about the subject

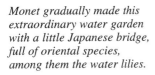

Monet gradually made this extraordinary water garden with a little Japanese bridge, full of oriental species, among them the water lilies.

as he was. However, Monet was not a chatterbox and he kept his artistic opinions for his closest friends: "The motif is insignificant to me; what I want to reproduce is what there is between the motif and me."

Hostile to Gauguin and anxious about the new trends developed by Seurat and Signac, he did not take part in the eighth Impressionist exhibition in 1886. He preferred to travel to Holland at the invitation of the Baron d'Estournelles de Constant, a friend of Deudon, one of his collectors. Going to see the fields of tulips in bloom was a fashionable excursion, but "a subject to drive a poor painter mad," as Monet said, delighted by those "rafts of color with yellow stains meeting the blue reflection of the sky." It was at the international exhibition organized by Georges Petit that his Dutch canvases were hung with other paintings from Menton and Étretat.

In the same year 1886, Durand-Ruel made his onslaught on the American market with an exhibition entitled "Oils and pastels by the Impressionists of Paris." Altogether three hundred paintings, forty-eight of which were by Monet, who was braced for a failure. But the American critics reacted positively, and the initiative marked the beginning of a craze for his work on the other side of the Atlantic.

In a letter to Boudin in 1889, on the occasion of the death of his friend's wife, Monet described his everyday life: "I am always in the country, often travelling, and constantly passing through Paris." That passion for the countryside inspired him to buy a plot of land at the mouth of the Epte. It was there that Suzanne Hoschedé posed for two versions of *Woman with a Sunshade* (1886). He repeated the layout he had used with Camille and Jean on a hill in Argenteuil, but laid on the colors with a fury that foreshadowed Fauvism.

The search for new motifs involved frequent travel. In September 1886 he discovered Belle-Île. Used to the storms of the Channel, which at Étretat almost swept him away from the slope where he was painting one day, Monet was both baffled and excited by the titanic fury of the ocean. "The gusts of wind sometimes tear his palette and brushes out of his hands. His easel is battened down with ropes and stones," wrote his future biographer, Gustave Geffroy. This contributor to *La Justice*, Clemenceau's journal, forged new links between the painter and the politician which would last until their deaths.

Photograph of Monet painting in his garden at Giverny, published by L'Intransigeant. *The painter of water and reflections said that "the essential thing about the motif is the mirror of water, whose appearance changes constantly because of the patches of sky reflected in it which fill it with life and movement."*

Presented at the International Exhibition of 1887 at Petit's gallery, where Renoir, Berthe Morisot, and Sisley followed him, the Belle-Île canvases breathe an extraordinary joy and vitality.

In August a short trip to London (where he was to return briefly the following year) led him to exhibit, on the recommendation of the chairman, Whistler, at the Royal Society of British Artists.

The savage brutality of the Atlantic was contrasted with the gentleness of the Mediterranean, which Monet rediscovered in 1888 at Antibes, at the Château de la Pinède, recommended by Maupassant who was staying at Cannes at the time.

The ten Antibes canvases were not shown by Durand-Ruel, with whom Monet was on distant terms, but by Théo Van Gogh (Vincent's brother), who managed the branch of Boussod-Valadon (formerly the house of Goupil, so famous abroad), in the Boulevard Montmartre. They were later acquired by American collectors, to the despair of Mirbeau. For his part, the critic Félix Fénéon, the neo-Impressionists' storm trooper, was not pleased by Monet's growing success: "Helped by an excessive bravura in the execution, a fertile improvization, and a brilliant vulgarity, his fame is on the increase."

The painter was well aware of that tendency towards the facile. He tried to put a brake on it in 1887 with his attempts at figures in the open air posed for by the young Hoschedé girls, and by returning to themes from Argenteuil. "It has occupied me until it has almost made me ill," he confided to Duret. Indeed, his bursts of intensive work were followed by periods of discouragement. That was still the case in 1889, in the early days of his stay at Fresselines in the Creuse with the poet Maurice Rollinat. "I follow nature but I can't capture it." But suddenly, with the coming of spring, Monet did not have a moment to lose; the barber even had to cut his hair while he carried on painting by the side of the rushing waters.

At the age of 49, he was now a personality in artistic life. Not only in France, but in the United States, where Sargent and Mary Cassatt introduced his work to their friends, and in London where the branch of Boussod-Valadon was showing twenty of his canvases under the title "Impressions". At the Universal Exhibition of 1889 three of his paintings appeared: *The Church at Vernon, The Tuileries, Vétheuil*. But his true moment of glory came, when in the same year, Georges Petitto grandiloquently linked his name with that of Auguste Rodin for an exhibition which brought together "the two giants of modern art." At the gallery in the Rue de Sèze, 36 sculptures by Rodin were shown alongside 145 canvases by Monet, done between 1864 and 1889. The first public appearance of the *Burghers of Calais* was a major event. It partly hid a canvas by Monet, which embittered and exasperated the painter who considered it a lack of delicacy on the part of Rodin. 1890 was largely occupied by a large-scale project: to get Manet's *Olympia* into the Louvre. "I am exasperated," wrote Monet, "by the silence and the injustice of everyone over his memory and his great talent." Sargent told him that one of his fellow countrymen was planning to buy the painting which no one had wanted at the sale after his death in 1884. Monet tripled his efforts to organize a subscription to buy the painting from Manet's widow for 20,000 francs. The initiative did not go down well with everyone; some people saw it as a form of self-advertising for Monet. Such was the opinion of Zola, whom the painter had cold-shouldered since the publication of *L'Œuvre* (The Work). Antonin

Proust, Manet's oldest friend, found the gesture insulting to the family; a duel was only narrowly avoided. In the end, in 1890 the National Museums Board accepted *Olympia* for the Musée du Luxembourg, which Clemenceau, in fulfillment of Monet's vow, transferred to the Louvre in 1907.

During the summer of 1890, Monet had given an old landscape, *Jeufosse*, to Mallarmé who had come to visit him at Giverny with Eugène Manet and his wife. It was Berthe Morisot who persuaded him to offer the painting in exchange for an illustration, still postponed, for the poem *Tiroir de Laque* (The Lacquer Drawer). Indeed, he had once again been gripped by doubt. He confided to Geffroy: "I am in the doldrums and totally sick of painting." Concerned about his state of depression, Mirbeau advised him not to "martyrize himself by wanting the impossible." Other worries came to trouble the artist's work. His son Jean had been afflicted with a serious illness during his military service. To have him discharged, Monet had to ask the help of Mallarmé, Bracquemond, Hanoteaux (director at the Foreign Ministry), and the painter Jeanniot, a friend of Degas.

However, his flourishing financial situation made it possible for him to buy his house in Giverny in the autumn of 1890. He was also able to build a new studio and create the garden of his dreams, which transformed his vision.

The 1890s marked a new direction. Monet had always liked to depict the same motif from different angles, in the manner of Hokusai or Hiroshige, of whom he was one of the earliest admirers. Now isolated compositions were a rarity. The time of the "series" had begun with

Monet photographed in the studio at his house in Giverny. The artist's canvases cover most of the walls and the picture windows open onto the wonders of the garden.

their variations in light or form and the unprecedented plastic nature of the impressions.

The first series was devoted to the *Stacks of Wheat* in winter or summer, alone or in groups, at sunrise or sunset. They were begun in the open air in the fields of Giverny and finished in the studio. In May 1891 of the twenty-two canvases shown by Durand-Ruel, fifteen were of haystacks. The exhibition was a triumph: "Everybody wants *Stacks of Wheat at Sunset*. Everything he does goes to America," wrote Pissarro. To America, where in New York in 1891, he had his first one-man exhibition, soon followed by another in Boston. Two years later, he had a further success in Chicago at the Columbus Centenary Exhibition, on which the fabulously wealthy Mrs. Potter Palmer had unstintingly lavished money.

In 1891 a new series was devoted to the *Poplars* on the Limetz marshes seen from a boat on the Epte. Among the twenty-three canvases, the ones depicting the tree trunks casting their reflections on the water strike us with the expressiveness of their color combinations, very close to Van Gogh. Once again they were a great success. Monet's financial situation now allowed him to withdraw Durand-Ruel's exclusivity, though he exhibited fifteen in 1892. However, in spite of his growing fame, his candidature in the same year for the decoration of the North and South Galleries of the Hôtel de Ville came to nothing. The commission was awarded to one Lagarde by ten votes to four.

In his family life, the death of Ernest Hoschedé in 1891 made it possible for him to regularize his situation a year later by marrying Alice, to whom he wrote in April 1889: "My only concern, my life, is Art and you." At the wedding, on 16 July 1892, the witnesses were Léon Monet,

Monet, Alice, and Clemenceau, the painter's intimate friend until his death. "Clemenceau, always so loyal, comes to see me often. Talking about something different seems to do him good, and at the same time, he comforts me. What a man!"

Pagny (Alice's brother-in-law), Helleu, and Caillebotte. It took place a few days before Suzanne Hoschedé's wedding to Theodore Butler, a painter and member of the American colony who had discovered Giverny some time before in the hope of meeting Monet or finding inspiration in the same landscapes. Some of them, such as Robinson and Lilla Perry, would be forever linked with the Monet-Hoschedés.

The theme of the third series – the procedure had become systematic – was Rouen Cathedral. In that town where his brother and the great collector Depeaux lived, Monet settled for two months beginning in February 1892 at the Hôtel d'Angleterre and rented a room at a novelty shop across the street from the masterpiece of Gothic architecture. A second visit for the same length of time in 1893 resulted in twenty-eight versions from three barely different angles, which he finished in his studio in Giverny. "The more I go the harder I find it to render what I feel and I tell myself that anyone who says he has finished a canvas is terribly proud,"

he wrote at the time. In spring and summer, often in the company of Blanche Hoschedé, the painter returned to former motifs: willows, poplars, mist on the Seine.

In the autumn of 1894 Cézanne, who was staying at the inn in Giverny, met Rodin, Clemenceau, and Geffroy, who had been recommended to him by his colleague. "Monet is the strongest of us all," said Cézanne, and ten years later he repeated : "I despise all living painters, except Renoir and Monet."

In artistic Paris, everyone was talking about nothing but the *Cathedrals*. About their unprecedented beauty, but also about their price. In the course of simultaneous negotiations with Durand-Ruel, the house of Boussod-Valadon and Maurice Joyant, Monet obtained 12,000 francs per canvas. The painter wanted to show the whole series together to the public and they first appeared in May 1895 at Durand-Ruel's gallery; of the 50 works on show, 20 were *Cathedrals*. Clemenceau voiced the general admiration by publishing in *La Justice* an article entitled "La Révolution des *Cathédrales*."

On the same occasion the visitors discovered eight Norwegian landscapes; Monet had spent two months there in the winter of 1895. He stayed with his son-in-law Jacques Hoschedé and was received as the "greatest landscape painter of the period." It was at Sandviken, at the house of the daughter-in-law of the dramatist Björnstjerne Björnson, that he found the motifs he brought back: red houses in the snow or views of Mount Kolsaas, brutal works which prefigured Fauvism. In his absence, Berthe Morisot had died of a severe attack of flu. A year before, Georges de Bellio and Caillebotte had died. In the legacy left

Monet with the Duke of Trévise in 1920, in front of the central part of the damaged canvas, Le Déjeuner sur l'Herbe. *The painter is exhibiting in his studio this emblematic fragment of the painting with which, sixty years before, he had made his first attempt at a response to the debate about modernism.*

to the nation by Caillebotte were sixteen works by Monet, but the painter disowned certain canvases which he judged unworthy of being hung in the Louvre.

His price tag continued to rise: 21,000 francs for *The Bridge at Argenteuil* in 1897. New dealers appeared, such as Bernheim junior, who in February 1902, hung *Mornings on the Seine*. In the face of the endless demand, he returned to his favorite places to rediscover motifs which he had already treated, partly adopting the series principle: at Pourville, Dieppe, and Varengeville between 1893 and 1897, and at Vétheuil in 1901, where he was accompanied by Jeanne Sisley, Alfred's daughter, as he had promised his old friend, who had died in 1899, that he would not abandon his family. The Universal Exhibition in 1900 was the apotheosis of Impressionism and the glory of Monet, represented at the show by fourteen paintings done at Argenteuil, Vétheuil, in Holland, in Normandy, and at Antibes.

Since 1890 gardening had occupied an increasingly important place in his life, especially the "water garden", which involved diverting a branch of the Epte. He was assisted by a head gardener and his team. The Japanese dealer and collector Hayashi, with whom he exchanged pictures for prints, sent rare species from his country. Monet was delighted by the water lilies celebrated by Mallarmé in a poem written in 1885, and to take better advantage of their blooming he built a bridge across the pond which seems to be straight out of a picture by Hokusai. The fragile structure appears in the first *Water Lilies* exhibited at Georges Petit's gallery in 1898. Two years later, Durand-Ruel showed a dozen canvases inspired by the same Japanese bridge and the clusters of willows and iris around it.

Nevertheless, the painter felt the need to offer his enthusiasts themes connected with the city and so turned his steps to London, which he had never ceased to admire. He spent the autumn of 1899 there, February 1990, and April 1991. His correspondence evokes a hundred or so canvases devoted to the *Houses of Parliament* (from St Thomas's hospital), *Charing Cross Bridge,* and *Waterloo Bridge* (seen from his room at the Savoy Hotel). The Thames, sparkling in the mist, plays a major part and gave the title to the exhibition at Durand-Ruel's gallery, "Views of the Thames in London," (37 canvases presented from 9 May to 4 June 1904). Those mists vibrant with light, where the influence of Turner and Whistler can be discerned, delighted lovers of Impressionism, while the new generation, which only had eyes for Cézanne and preached a return to geometry, remained indifferent.

His last journey abroad was to Venice, where he was accompanied by Alice in the autumn of 1908. Like all painters before him he left images of the Doges' Palace, the Salute, and the Grand Canal. The works were collected in an exhibition at Bernheim's in 1912.

On the way back, Monet stopped to visit one of his stepdaughters in Cagnes and went to see Renoir at Les Collettes. Since the death of Cézanne in 1906, they were, with Degas, the great survivors of the Impressionist generation. The rumor of their glory preceded them everywhere and every subject they tackled drew flocks of admirers.

The water garden with which he seems to have carried on an uninterrupted dialogue occupied an essential place in Monet's work from 1904 to 1908. Since 1902 the bridge motif had disappeared. The painter's eye now rested only on the beds of iris and lilies and the rippling surface where the reflections of the clouds blend with those of the water lilies.

Four dozen water landscapes were collected in 1909 at Durand-Ruel's gallery. The critic Roger Marx hoped that some patron would make a single, uninterrupted decoration with them. It was Clemenceau who made that dream come true. He often came from his house at Bernouville to Giverny, where visitors were ever more numerous: hungry collectors – like Paul Gallimard, Raymond Kœchlin, the jeweller Vever – personalities from literature or the theatre: among them Paul Valéry, Sacha Guitry, and the singer Namara; and painters: Signac, Bonnard, and Vuillard.

1911 to 1914 was a painful time. The painter lost his wife Alice in 1911; then in 1914 his son Jean, who had married Blanche Hoschedé in 1897. It took all the devoted attention of his daughter-in-law, who had come to live with him at Giverny, and that of his close friends Clemenceau and Geffroy, to help him rediscover his taste for painting and to return to the project for the large decorative works on the theme of the *Water Lilies*. Apart from his two studios, a third one equipped with overhead lighting, was built specially for the purpose. Rising at four in the morning, as he had done all his life, Monet covered his great surfaces frantically. Once again it was Clemenceau who suggested that he should contribute to the victory celebrations of 1918 by offering the *Water Lilies* to the nation. After the donation, which was made in 1922, a room at the Orangerie des Tuileries was specially prepared to house them. Since Monet had not wished to be separated from them in his lifetime, the collection of nineteen panels was only opened in May 1927.

After 1912, while continuing to paint, he began to complain of eye problems which increasingly troubled his sight. In 1923 a cataract operation restored it to him and allowed him to return to work with his customary ardor. He died on 5 December 1926 at the age of 86. At his funeral, the faithful Clemenceau paid him a last tribute. He rejected the black drape intended to cover the coffin and replaced it with a flowered one, declaring: "No black for Monet."

In the nineteen-twenties, Monet continued to work on the water lilies series and said: "Immersed in my work, I forget about everything, because I feel happy to have finally rediscovered the vision of colors. It has been a true resurrection."

HUNTING TROPHY, 1862
Oil on canvas, 104 x 75 cm
Musée d'Orsay, Paris

HUNTING TROPHY

Monet was still signing with the initial of his first name, Oscar, on this bravura piece done before he entered the Gleyre studio.

At the Salon of 1859 he had admired "a really beautiful picture by Troyon, a dog with a partridge in its mouth." Moreover, his mentor, Boudin, had done some still lifes with game a few years earlier.

The increased wealth of the bourgeoisie under the Second Empire had brought back a kind of decorative, family painting, dignified in the 18th century by Chardin, Oudry, and Desportes. Subjects of that kind were easy for a young painter to sell, and Monet must also have seen examples by

Charles Monginot, who lent him his studio in 1859 and 1860. A pupil of Couture and an intimate friend of Monet, he eventually specialized in the genre. Antwerp Museum still has one of his *Hunting Trophies*. The young Monet also did some more realistic still lifes at that time, doubtless inspired by François Bouvin, whom he met at the Brasserie des Martyrs, or by Théodule Ribot, a regular at the Auberge Saint-Siméon in Honfleur. His layout of this hunting trophy is superb and he probably showed it to his future teacher as proof of his skills. In this slightly off-center pyramidal composition the powder horn stands out against the light wall. The diagonal of the rifle cuts through the triangle formed by the

straps of the cartridge belt. The soberness of the woodwork is contrasted with the pile of feathered game on the red marble hunting table and the spaniel in the foreground gazes in fascination at the sight. Monet has detailed with an extraordinary brio the golden pheasant, the grouse outlined against the game pouch, the red partridge, the woodcock and the snipe. But there was to be no sequel to this beautiful demonstration, and it was not in this kind of subject that he made his career later on.

THE PICNIC, 1865-1866
Oil on canvas, (central part)
248 x 217 cm
Musée d'Orsay, Paris

THE PICNIC

"I no longer think of anything but my picture and if I thought I was going to fail, I think I would go mad," Monet wrote to Bazille. He was twenty-five years old and daring in every respect. He chose an exceptional format (6 x 4.60 m), usually reserved for the "big" historical and religious subjects and not for an entertainment as banal as a picnic. To plunge into the representation of so many life-size figures was an ambitious challenge for a young artist who had still not painted groups. After showing his skill with typical Barbizon landscapes, such as *Le Pavé de Chailly* and some solid seascapes, he had now made up his mind to strike a major blow and impose himself at the next Salon.

Monet knew that Bruyas, the collector he was hoping to interest through the mediation of Bazille, owned a *Picnic* by Glaize. He was also well aware of Courbet's success in Germany with the *Huntsmen's Breakfast* he had painted in Frankfurt. From April to October he worked at Chailly, drawing figures and using young friends as models. He insisted on Bazille coming: "I would like your advice about the choice of landscape for my figures, I am sometimes afraid of making a blunder."

As it was not finished in time, the painting was not presented at the Salon. Worse still, in 1878 Monet had to leave it as security to the landlord of his house in Argenteuil. When he recovered it in 1884, the damp had rotted several pieces of the canvas. What remains today are the left-hand part (Musée d'Orsay), showing the arrival of three guests, and the center of the painting, reproduced here. A final study (Pushkin Museum, Moscow) shows the overall composition. Unlike Manet, who in his *Déjeuner sur l'herbe* had painted the nude and the superb still life in the light of the studio, Monet placed the figures and the food in the foreground in real daylight. He innovated radically by using those blotches of sunlight which give the canvas its original tonality, so much so that it marks a crucial moment in modern art.

The immaculate cloth with its sunlit patches and the young woman in dotted white muslin create a lozenge of light in the undergrowth, which is treated more freely than in his *Oak at Bodmer*. The scene is focussed on the bottles, the peaches, and grapes caressed by the sun. The bread, the chicken, and the pie, an appetizing golden brown, make the mouth water. The original work had twelve figures. There are only four in the fragment we are looking at, and on either side, the invisible presence of women of whom all that remains is a piece of clothing. In the

background we recognize Bazille, who had posed for several male figures. The slim Lambron des Piltières, the original model for the seated man, had been replaced by Courbet, who had come to see Monet while he was working. In a photo taken in 1920 at Giverny, we see on the right the head of a woman wearing a feathered hat. She has disappeared. Was it Camille, who it is believed, came into Monet's life on the occasion of this picture? There too Monet is different from Manet. There is nothing licentious about the atmosphere, nothing ambiguous; just conviviality. The artist is trying mainly to capture the instantaneous quality of the scene. All the actors are performing a movement. The man in the black suit, streaked with blue reflections, is holding out his glass; his neighbor is reaching for a plate; behind them the young woman is removing her hat, while her companion is about to put down the yellow sunshade and the pale blue shawl she has handed him. Around them the clearing breathes at its own rhythm as it opens up to this friendly company; the ritual of the picnic may begin.

Jeanne-Marguerite Lecadre in the Garden, 1867
Oil on canvas, 80 x 99 cm
The Hermitage Museum, St. Petersburg

Jeanne-Marguerite Lecadre in the Garden

Sainte-Adresse, close by Le Havre, the summer residence of the bourgeoisie of the great port, was made fashionable by Alphonse Karr. His *Evenings at Sainte-Adresse* (1853) and his books about his Norman garden had been best sellers. Monet undoubtedly owes him the choice of this theme in the summer of 1867 when he had been reconciled with his family and was staying with his aunt, Marie-Jeanne Lecadre, the widow of a wholesale grocer and ships' chandler. "Each brushstroke is admirable," he told his friends in reference to the works he was doing at the time, and added that his friend Guillemet, who had come to see him, "had been stunned."
Those canvases show the two faces of Sainte-Adresse: the sea (*The Terrace at Sainte-Adresse*) and the countryside. It was at Le Coteau, the property of Doctor Auguste Lecadre, his aunt's nephew, that Monet painted this bourgeois garden with its carefully tended lawn, lightly spotted with daisies, and protected from prying eyes and the wind by a thick hedge of walnut trees. "Claude Monet has a

particular love for nature which the hand of man has dressed up in modern style," wrote Zola in *L'Événement Illustré* on 24 May 1868. The novelist, who had seen his garden canvases, regretted the rejection by the jury of the Salon, but "what does it matter?" he thought, "they will remain among the great curiosities of our time." Indeed the authority with which Monet places the masses of greenery, stretches out the shadows and adds the scarlet of the flowers and the dense blue of the summer sky makes the work quite different from others of the same kind accepted by the Salon, whether the slightly fragile young women by Toulmouche, a cousin of the Lecadres, or the seductive *Young Women in a Park* by Tissot, a friend of Degas. They were painting portraits; Monet is evoking a presence, that of Jeanne-Marguerite

Lecadre, one of the three daughters of Doctor Lecadre, but as a decorative element in a horticultural universe. Preeminence goes to the garden: a bed of geraniums crowned with a cascade of white roses, great trees mingled with poplars, a distant flower-bed fenced with rose stalks. The varnished foliage of an exotic Indian shrub tells us that we are in Le Havre, a city where amateur gardeners fought over the species brought from overseas. There is no way of recognizing the woman strolling, a simple silhouette in a state of weightlessness on the grass. She comes on stage, as in the theatre. And from that moment there is an imposed comparison between the dazzling "queen of the snows" rose bush in the center of the composition and the erect young woman walking towards it, dressed in the same spotless white as the flowers.

WOMEN IN THE GARDEN, 1866-1867
Oil on canvas, 255 x 205 cm
Musée d'Orsay, Paris

WOMEN IN THE GARDEN

These *Women in the Garden* seem to be straight out of *The Picnic*. Three of them are wearing identical dresses to the ones in the other picture. They move in the luminous warmth of an ornamental garden.

Here again Monet sets the figures in a landscape and the format, though smaller, is still substantial. The work was undertaken after the success of *Camille* at the Salon and was intended to allow the painter to face the next jury with a pleasing subject which always went down well: women and flowers.

Winterhalter in official mode, and Stevens in a more bourgeois manner, set the example. Bazille paid the considerable sum of 2,500 francs for this picture painted in one of his gardens at Ville-d'Avray, which Victorien Sardou describes in his plays.

Painting in the open air, recommended by Boudin, is as important here as Monet always claimed in his arguments, which at times verged on advertising. He had a trench dug in his garden which allowed him to raise or lower the canvas as he chose according to the part he was working on, restoring the impalpable atmosphere of a summer afternoon in all its spontaneity: the rustling of the trees and the vibration of the light, the clash of shadows and colors.

The work was started at the villa Monet had rented at Sèvres-Ville-d'Avray and finished in winter in the Cheval Blanc studio in Honfleur. In this depthless composition the silhouettes around the central tree form a kind of roundabout which exudes charm and lightness. Like Baudelaire, Monet "is avenging the art of painting clothes for the inept slanders heaped on it by certain questionable nature lovers." Camille's curved silhouette appears on the left in a green and white striped dress and a tiny, flat, flowered hat with a "follow-me-lads" ribbon hanging at the

back. It is her again, facing us in the peach colored dress and hiding her face behind a bouquet of roses, poppies, anemones, and camomiles. It is unlikely that she posed for the sitting woman, whose features are those of the model who occupies the central place in *The Picnic*.
Her dress flares out like the cup of a flower. Women/flowers and women/flower-

Courrier élégant must have damaged this canvas in the eyes of the jury, who rejected it in 1867. A year later, Zola remarked: "(Monet) loves our women, their sunshades, their gloves, their ribbons, even their hairpieces and their toilet powder, everything that makes them girls of our civilization... Like a true Parisian, he takes Paris to the country. He is incapable of painting a landscape without putting

sellers, a profession which some of his friends had practiced, Pissarro and Zola's companions, for example.
Slightly apart from the others, a young girl is leaning towards the rose bush in a turning movement that enhances the flow of the material. A certain similarity with the fashion engravings in the *Journal des Demoiselles* or the

in ladies and gentlemen dressed up in their best..." And, indignant over the rejection of *Women in the Garden*, he insisted: "One has to be particularly fond of one's own day and age to attempt a *tour de force* like this, fabrics sliced in two by the shadows and the sunlight."

GARDEN AT SAINTE-ADRESSE OR THE TERRACE AT SAINTE-ADRESSE, 1866-1867
Oil on canvas, 98 x 130 cm
The Metropolitan Museum of Art, New York

GARDEN AT SAINTE-ADRESSE OR THE TERRACE AT SAINTE-ADRESSE

"Some astonishing seascapes and figures and gardens." Monet enthusiastically listed to Bazille the subjects he was working on. This picture in fact belonged to a friend of his. *Garden at Sainte-Adresse* is probably the name under which it was exhibited in 1879, but the title *The Terrace at Sainte-Adresse* which it bore for long afterwards is infinitely more significant. All is mystery in this picture, though its brilliance seems to be hiding nothing – not only the title, but also the protagonists. We think we can recognize Adolphe Monet, the painter's father, but is the woman sitting at his side his half-sister, Marie-Jeanne Lecadre or Sophie, Doctor Lecadre's wife? The painter juxtaposes two worlds which are familiar to him: the bourgeoisie of Le Havre and the commercial activity of the great port. Two spaces separated by a barrier, linked by the eyes of the figures and the painter: the intimacy of the terrace is contrasted with the immensity of the sea; both seem calm, quite different from the undergrowth of Chailly or the dynamism of *The Green Wave* (1865).
"My Chinese picture with the flags," said Monet to identify this canvas. It shows the brand new influence of the prints brought from Japan and also that there was still some confusion about the terminology for things

Chinese and things Japanese. The freshness of the colors and the absence of any passage between them correspond to everything that delighted artists in the prints which were on show at the Universal Exhibition in 1867. Ernest Chesneau describes the motifs, taken from an elevated point "so that the different planes are established by their height. In that way, without having recourse to aerial perspective, the difference of proportion is enough to establish the illusion of real perspective." Monet has put parallel bands staged in the same way. Between the blue of the sky and the cobalt of the waves stretches a horizon where the pale clouds blend with the pale smoke of the ships.

In the foreground, in the quadrilateral marked out by the balustrade and the flower-beds, an invisible but pervasive sun picks out each element sharply: the rectangle and triangle of the pennants, the curve of the chestnut armchairs, the verticals of the masts which are echoed by the stems of the gladioli. We can already recognize the fanatical amateur gardener that Monet was to become in the pleasure he takes in describing the crimson bloom of the nasturtiums, geraniums, and poppies; the white of the daisies; the gray of the cineraria. The flowers and chairs describe the arc of a circle, like the balcony of a theatre, where the stage is occupied by the two people chatting by the balustrade. We do not know if the elderly couple are keeping an eye on the young people or if they are watching on the horizon the parade of ships to which they owe their prosperity as big traders in groceries for the navy. An impression of summer and aesthetic perfection stands out from this sunbathed panorama. A solitary black sailboat seems to be becalmed on a sea barely ruffled by a slight lapping of the waves. In the distance the great three-masted schooners and the steamboats bound for America precede a flotilla making out to sea. The variety of boats embodies the variety of activities of Le Havre – fishing, trade, leisure – revealing the painter's purpose: to create a modern work, a manifesto of contemporary life, thus following Manet's watchword, "One must be up to date."

ROUGH SEA AT ÉTRETAT,
1868-1869
Oil on canvas, 66 x 131 cm
Musée d'Orsay, Paris

ROUGH SEA AT ÉTRETAT

At Étretat, another resort launched by Alphonse Karr, Monet rented a house thanks to the generosity of Gaudibert, his first patron. He was following in the footsteps of artists he admired. Delacroix had painted the same cliffs when he visited his cousins in Valmont, and Corot worked there in 1864 under the observant eye of Maupassant. A work by Monet called *The Cliff* is very close to a watercolor by Eugène Isabey, the friend who showed Jongkind Normandy. Paul Huet was there in 1868, shortly before Monet, and

Courbet, who took him to see the beautiful Ernestine, painted the famous *Wave* the following year. Monet's waves have a different spirit; they are both more expressive and more colored.

Brought to life in summer by a sophisticated crowd of novelists, among them Dumas "fils", or actors; in winter the resort became a fishing village again.

Ships Leaving the Jetties of Le Havre, which had just been purchased by the Gaudiberts, had been much commented on at the Salon. A caricaturist had even made a play of words on the painter's name and his speed of interpretation by labelling his cartoon "Go ahead, time is money." That speed of execution, for which he was reproached by some people, was applied by Monet even more in this canvas of Étretat.

We see here for the first time, though without any

special emphasis, the cliff which later inspired so many masterpieces. "Here I am surrounded by everything I like," he wrote in one of his letters, "... I spend my time in the open air on the shingle when the weather is rough or when the fishing boats are sailing out." Those boats appear in several of his canvases as they sail out to sea, rocking slowly on the waves. As for the scene represented here, he has observed it from the top of the path down to the sea; the drawing is in one of his sketchbooks.

The waves are breaking, heavily topped with white, leaving just a narrow strip of beach on which a group of men and women are watching them roll in. Old fishermen, wives, and children brought together by the same anxiety, this could be a genre painting of the kind exhibited since Victor Hugo published

The Toilers of the Sea and put the anguish of that life in verse in *Océano Nox*. But Monet never takes the easy way. A dense paste brings a surprising vigor to the picture. The figures, barely outlines, speak volumes. A man scans the horizon with his hand over his eyes; women turn to each other, wondering. All of them racked with anxiety by that black point tossed by the waves at the edge of the ink-colored sky and the yellowish water, which should be the boat they are waiting for. A scene from everyday life in a fishing port, this dramatic wait could also refer to Swinburne.

The English poet, who lived at Étretat at the time in his cottage in Dolmancé, a name taken from Sade, almost drowned on this beach and owed his life to the lifeboat aboard which was Maupassant.

THE MAGPIE

This picture is one of Monet's absolute masterpieces. It proves that by 1869 the formidable interplay of values of white imposed by winter landscapes held no more secrets for him. "It was cold enough to split stone. We saw a brazier, then an easel, then a gentleman muffled up in three overcoats, gloved hands, his face half frozen: it was Monsieur Monet studying an effect

of snow." That first description of Monet at work tells the story of a meeting at Saint-Siméon, early in 1867. Monet was then painting his first «felicitous» snowy landscapes according to Dubourg, a friend of Boudin.
It seems that Courbet must have urged his young friend to tackle the subjects he painted himself with such delectation at Ornans. He must also have pointed out to him that art

lovers were clamoring for canvases like his *Watchful Roe Deer in Winter* (Lyon Museum, 1866). January 1869 was particularly snowy and cold (the Seine froze over). At Étretat, Monet prepared new winter subjects and thought of selling the ones he had already completed, since he mentioned to Bazille "an effect of pure white snow and a smaller one with crows." He also ordered paints of the kind we see in *The Magpie*:

THE MAGPIE, 1869
Oil on canvas, 89 x 130 cm
Musée d'Orsay, Paris

"Silver white, plenty, ivory black, plenty, cobalt blue, plenty, fine lake, ochre yellow...." He was going to use those different pigments to suggest the snow. Those are not the harmonies of white and brown of the skating scenes that Jongkind painted in

Honfleur from his memories of Holland. Not are they the heavy, dense snow of Courbet; they are an airy, luminous material. Monet's interest in Dutch painting, mentioned by Boudin, leads us to suppose that he was not unfamiliar with Brueghel's work. But while the Dutch master peoples his canvas with figures, Monet shows a world from which man is totally absent. This simple composition – Corot is not far away – with its wicker fence still woven as in the

I realize that we do not dare to express frankly what we feel. It's funny," he confided to Bazille. That winter light which makes the trees pink and the snow blue was unknown to the Parisians, snug in their apartments. If this work was one of the two rejected by the Salon in 1869, the only reason could be those admirable effects of blue shadows and their echo on the plumage of the magpie,

Middle Ages is perfectly balanced: a foreground given over to the geometry of the shadows, a second ground with the magic of the snow-covered branches, an immense horizon which could be a plain or the sea. "The more I work, the more

as if to accentuate that colorist determination which turns it into a blue bird, the color of the weather.

LA GRENOUILLÈRE, 1869
Oil on canvas, 74.6 x 99.7 cm
*The Metropolitan Museum of
Art (Gift of H.O. Havemeyer),
New York*

LA GRENOUILLÈRE

In July 1869, the visit of
Napoleon III and the
Empress Eugénie brought
a special glow to this
pleasure garden at the
dizzy height of fashion on
the Île de Croissy, across
from Bougival. It acted as
an immediate spur to
Monet, who had recently
moved in at Saint-Michel-
de-Bougival. At the next
Salon he was to exhibit a
view of La Grenouillère.
The project, which was not
crowned with success, also
seduced Renoir who was
staying not far away
with his parents, in
Louveciennes. Both of
them set up their easels on
the islet every day.
Writers, artists, publishers,
stockbrokers gathered at
this bathing establishment
accompanied by those
frivolous girls from Paris
whose taste for swimming
gave them the nickname
of "frogs" (grenouilles).
In their different versions
of La Grenouillère, the
intimately connected
landscapes and people no
longer serve to show each
other off; they convey the
"correspondences" so dear
to Baudelaire. Monet is
already drawn by his
fascination with water
towards complex
abstractions between the
reflections of the sky,
the line of the trees, the
nautical constructions, and
the figures. A major
element in the
composition, the Seine
displays all the sensations

of a beautiful summer afternoon on its surface. In the foreground, calm and coolness. Empty boats await the customers; their gentle rocking tinges the waves with horizontal touches, white, ultramarine, and ochre. In the shadow of the floating café whose balustrade bears the legend "Location de canots" (boats for hire) the crimson reflection of the edge of the boat streaks the water.

The closer we come to the islet, the closer the colors come together and, in the space reserved for the bathing, the values become lighter, accentuating the ripples. In the distance we can barely make out a few boats passing along the far bank and the almost stylized vegetation with shades that herald the end of summer.

All the lines of the boats, the gangways, and the café converge on the islet, known as "the camembert" or "the flower pot". The central tree casts its shadow towards the edge of the picture, the very spot where the painter must be standing.

In this composition, the elegant ladies of *The Picnic*, *Women in the Garden* or *The Terrace at Sainte-Adresse* have disappeared. No faces can be seen. Manet, Degas, Sisley, the Stevens brothers who had a salon inside La Grenouillère, may be there among those barely sketched silhouettes, which form a succession of snapshots: figures standing in the bar, a man treading gingerly along the gangway, bathers rubbing shoulders with strollers whose barely detailed clothes take on the hues of the water.

A second version of the subject brings more animation to the islet and the Seine, on which boats are sailing. A third highlights the boats in the foreground and the gangway where the robust bathers are walking. The atmosphere is brought back to life by the pen of Maupassant, a regular at the spot like Tiburce Morisot, whose mother described this Grenouillère to her daughter Berthe: "They say it is a rather rustic meeting place for very frivolous people and if you go there alone you come back with at least one other person." Today the name is indissolubly linked with Renoir and Monet, for it was on this bank of the Seine that "the new painting," which had not yet been named Impressionism, began its meteoric rise.

THE HÔTEL DES ROCHES-
NOIRES , TROUVILLE, 1870
Oil on canvas, 81 x 58.5 cm
Musée d'Orsay, Paris

THE HÔTEL DES ROCHES-
NOIRES, TROUVILLE

The season was in full swing in Trouville that summer of 1870. On the beach, an extension of Deauville launched by the Duc de Morny, the beauties of the Second Empire were to be seen: Madame de Metternich, Madame de Galliffet, Madame de Pourtalès. The elegant sights of the resort had inspired Boudin over the years to paint some of his best loved pictures. A dealer, Gauchez, systematically bought up all his small subjects. In August Monet, exasperated by the rejection of *La Grenouillère* and *The Picnic* at the Salon of 1870, set off to join him, hoping to take advantage of the reigning enthusiasm. He stayed with Camille and their son at the Hôtel Tivoli in a back street in the town. But to paint he set up his easel in front of the sumptuous Hôtel des Roches-Noires, packed with celebrities. He immortalized it thirty years before it was used as a model, with the one in Cabourg, for the Hôtel de Balbec created by Marcel Proust in *Remembrance of Things Past*.
Although a letter from Bazille asked, "Is Monet painting Madame de Metternich?", the people are barely recognizable in the canvases painted in front of the Hôtel des Roches-Noires, and their silhouettes betray a more synthetic vision than Boudin's.
If the flags flying in the wind recall *The Terrace at Sainte-Adresse*, the style and the atmosphere are far away. The relentless light, the strict arrangement and the violence of the colors stand in sharp contrast to the gentle light

here: a summer sky with clouds against the blue of the vault and piled up on the horizon. Monet gives himself over to these climatic sensations, one of the bases of Impressionism.

An original layout which brings out the proud building in a retreating rather than a frontal perspective. On this palette which is all in shades, the light tonalities, where the beige color of the sand and the stone and the obligatory white dresses dominate, are broken only by a few touches of red. The family intimacy of Sainte-Adresse is countered by the summer bustle of Trouville: people arrive and depart, lean on their balconies, stroll, greet one another, and show themselves off, all with an aristocratic elegance. The show is not provided by the sea, which is scarcely visible, but by the comings and goings on the promenade alongside it. In the foreground a large empty space isolates the figures in this area closed on the one side by the line of lamps and flags and on the other by the imposing mass of the hotel. It is the floor for this worldly dance, delightful and frivolous, which the outbreak of war is about to interrupt.

WINDMILLS NEAR ZAANDAM, 1871
Oil on canvas, 40 x 72 cm
The Walters Art Gallery, Baltimore

WINDMILLS NEAR ZAANDAM

"There is enough here to paint for the rest of one's life," Monet told Pissarro when he arrived at Zaandam in Holland. He was returning from England, where several painters who had been exhibiting with him at Durand-Ruel's London gallery advised him to make the stopover. Legros, for example, or Bellet du Poisat, a friend of Degas' noticed at the Salon of 1870 for his views of Holland. The town, five miles from Amsterdam, was then considered one of the most original in Europe, and Jongkind had often boasted of its landscapes to his French colleagues. Monet found the Japan, which Van Gogh was to search for in Arles in the façades splashed with pinks, greens, and blues between the rows of elms and the humpbacked bridges. 254 windmills, of which Élisée Reclus engraved an illustration for his *Géographie universelle*, stood there in their diversity and strangeness.

For the first time the idea of a "series" appeared in Monet's painting and soon aroused the interest of his colleagues, as Henri-Michel Lévy, whom he met at Zaandam, and Daubigny would be among the first people to buy these scenes. In this picture from the Baltimore Museum, a sky with fleecy clouds, like in a painting by Constable, crushes the flat country of the polders. There is a hint of the style of Jacob Maris and the painters of the Hague School, which was highly appreciated in England. Canals and paths between Zaandam and Oostzaan stretch away to the horizon where the bell-tower of the Oostzijderkerk stands next to the sails of a windmill. A woman walks down the steps of the bridge. Her pointed headgear, the yoke holding up the buckets she is carrying, add a slight sociological connotation to what might pass for a pure landscape. Cropped grass, vague reflections of the water on which a boat is maneuvering in the distance. This picture distills an impression of extreme solitude; it may have been one of the first done by the painter on his arrival in Holland.

IMPRESSION, SUNRISE, 1872
Oil on canvas, 48 x 63 cm
Musée Marmottan, Paris

IMPRESSION, SUNRISE

A legendary work, the work which gave its name to the most popular movement in the history of painting, *Impression, Sunrise,* made its entry into that history in 1874. The public discovered it at the first collective exhibition of the so-called "Batignolles Group." We can read about their reaction to the work in the press of the day. Leroy, of *Le Charivari*, entitled his article "The Exhibition of the Impressionists", choosing *Impression* as a special target; for him "wallpaper at its embryonic stage is more finished than this seascape." Marc de Montifaud, the pseudonym of a woman reporter close to Nina de Callias and Villiers de l'Isle-Adam, friends of the artists in the group, saw in the picture "the hand of a child who is studying color for the first time."

On the other side, Philippe Burty was grateful to Monet for "fixing such fleeting impressions."

Armand Silvestre, another friend of the painters, compares Monet's vision with Pissarro's, and Sisley's and explains, "It is indeed only an impression which it pursues, leaving the search for expression to lovers of line." The resemblance of the painting to a watercolor was also mentioned. That must have appealed to Ernest Hoschedé, its first buyer, who had been noted since before 1870, along with Monsieur de Boissieu, as a collector who brought the technique back into fashion. On its sale in 1878, Doctor Bellio became the owner for 210 francs.

Today we can better understand the intentions behind this picture done by the painter at the Hôtel de l'Amirauté in Le Havre. His window overlooked the inner harbor which was destroyed in the Second World War. He made different interpretations at different times of night and day. This one fixes the most fleeting instant, when the sun emerges from the mist. At the same time his procedure leaves the material of the canvas on view, as if to emphasize the speed inherent to its execution. There is nothing fortuitous about this pictorial space, however; there is a coherent construction in successive planes: water, boats, sky. It transmutes earlier influences into something new and barbarous. That sun that darts its streak of fire at the surface of the water Monet had seen in the work of Jongkind and had discovered in Turner's watercolors of the

Rigi or Petworth, which also have the same sky washed with a thousand pinks.

His *Impression*, at first simply entitled *Marine*, owed its final, most convincing name to Edmond Renoir, who pressed Monet for a more precise title for the catalogue. It exactly restores the feeling of the ephemeral linked to an in-between time of day when the smoke contaminates the color of the clouds and the masts take on the colors of the water. But it is not the atmospheric, instantaneous quality which Baudelaire admired in Boudin. For the first time a painter offers a transcription by sign rather than by image. This makes us wonder about the Chinese and Japanese paintings which Monet had seen in England and Holland. He could not have been unaware of the Zen works (those by Sesshu for example), as his canvas illustrates the same search for spontaneity of movement and suggestive creation, which begun by the artist, must be finished in the mind of the spectator.

The painting thus becomes, as Pierre Daix wrote, "a spectacle being born in its unknown freshness and its blossoming colors. Taken by surprise. You have before you *Impression, Sunrise*."

Here we find various elements from other paintings: the arches of the road bridge, scarcely visible between two sails, and the little house with the dormer window and its tree on the bank. Jongkind's influence can be seen in the discontinuous treatment of the reflections. Moreover, during his stay in England he had discovered Turner's watercolors and the simplifications Whistler borrowed from the Japanese. The impact of those *Regattas* seems to refer back to the impression made by the Japanese prints on one of Goncourt's heroes: "A day in fairyland, a day without shadows which was only light, rose for him from

**REGATTAS
AT ARGENTEUIL,** 1872
Oil on canvas, 48 x 75 cm
Musée d'Orsay, Paris

REGATTAS AT ARGENTEUIL

Monet's life was ruled by a passion for boats. The presence of the Yachting Club de Paris in Argenteuil was undoubtedly one of the reasons why he settled there on his return from Holland. His childhood in Le Havre, so famous for its regattas, imbued him with

his love of this nautical sport. Not only did he practice it; he was delighted to represent this flight of sails at Sainte-Adresse and on the basin formed by the Seine between Argenteuil and Gennevilliers. His friends, Sisley, with *The Regattas at Hampton Court* (1874), and Caillebotte, a little later, followed his example.

On the Seine a floating studio allowed him to spot the motifs and sometimes to paint the same subject from different points of view. For this work he had moored his boat opposite Argenteuil, upriver on the Petit-Gennevilliers bank.

those albums of Japanese drawings." But here we can no longer speak of influence. The assimilation of Japanese art is such that an entirely new style imposes itself. The composition is all sobriety: a few sails, two houses, and a patch of river bank, almost in line, are cut out between sky and water. The background and foreground merge. The white and crimson strike out from the blues of the sky and the river, and the green of the bank. Violence, too, in the crude, almost blinding light. If the water dissolves the elements (houses, boats, trees, and even people), shattering what the brush has constructed into smithereens, it in no way dims the colors, thus bringing an intense life to the foreground. The broad, firm touches create a parallel floating universe on the surface of the water, no less present than the real world. As always, Monet depicts the discreet actors of the scene with a remarkable economy of resources: a woman with a sunshade near the house or the men handling the sailboats. Crude colors, violent images, *Regattas at Argenteuil* heralds Fauvism thirty years before its time.

POPPIES AT ARGENTEUIL, 1873
Oil on canvas, 50 x 65 cm
Musée d'Orsay, Paris

POPPIES AT ARGENTEUIL

The surroundings of Argenteuil – the banks of the Seine, the fields, and hills – provide a variety of landscapes and light which Monet and his friends never ceased to paint. Thus, while he was staying with him, Renoir did a *Path through the Long Grass*, which is very close to these *Poppies at Argenteuil*.

What they were attempting to convey was not the landscape but the feelings it produced, as Castagnary explains in his definition of the new painting. The innovative aspect of this small-format picture, which was presented at the first Impressionist exhibition, is obvious if we compare it with *Fields in June* by Daubigny, a large canvas with a more classical handling, shown at the Salon in 1873. *Picnic at the Temple of Kaian to Admire the Red Maples at Shinagawa,* the print by Hiroshige which Monet owned, may have

inspired this presentation of the figures in two groups. The fact of showing Camille and their son hurrying out of the field of vision, while their doubles are outlined on the horizon, punctuates the scene and gives it its movement and instantaneous quality. The simplicity of the composition – a house framed by trees, a field of poppies crossed by figures, and an empty space – gives the canvas a radiant lightness. It is no less animated by underlying lines which bring out a host of trajectories for the eye and as many possible walks for the painter.

A diagonal on the left rises towards a gap in the trees from which the strollers have emerged; a perpendicular leads to the Mill of Orgemont, distant but very much present. In the center and on the right, sinuous lines marked by the turbulence of the touch – broad or thin, vertical or horizontal – and by the variations of a green that ranges from brown to khaki and is sometimes covered with sheets of gray and purple, hint at hidden paths. They also suggest the intense life going on beneath these rustling grasses, even if they do not provide the same blaze as the poppies next to them.

A sky streaked with white clouds adds still more to the light rising from the scarlet carpet from which the walkers are emerging. Little Jean, with his bouquet and the red ribbon on his hat, almost merges with the flowers. Camille, always elegant in her black shawl and her dress which blends into the meadow, has abandoned the tiny hats she wore before 1870 in favor of a kind that offers better protection for her complexion. Very "Parisienne in the countryside," she walks nonchalantly and gracefully, toying with a sunshade in subtle blues. A feeling of slow motion, of time in suspension, reigns in this field enclosed by a barrier of trees. An image of a protected world where the red of the poppies is there, as if to recall that only just before, men had been dying on the battlefields of Argenteuil or the barricades of the Commune.

LUNCHEON, 1873-1874
Oil on canvas, 160 x 201 cm
Musée d'Orsay, Paris

LUNCHEON

Monet chose an unusual format for this work done while he was staying at Argenteuil and presented at the second Impressionist exhibition (1876) under the title *Decorative Panel*. The comparison with *Luncheon* done in 1868 in Étretat, where his son was represented at table with two female figures, shows the break between the painting of the pre-war years and the later canvases.

The realistic character of the family meal at Étretat is completely different from the totally unreal quality of this scene in the garden of the Aubry house which is both strange and familiar, immediate yet timeless. A strange title, indeed, for a lunch which no one is eating: neither the women in the light dresses walking in the background, or the child (Jean Monet) concentrating on his building game. Only

the symbolic choice of the objects composes a refined still life and tells us that a meal has just taken place after a stroll on the banks of the Seine or through the poppy fields.

The foreground is given over to the abandoned table and the wicker stand, cut off like the bench, by a Degas style layout.

The food (a fruit bowl of peaches, a plate of plums, broken bread), the crockery (porcelain cups, silver coffee pot, two glasses with a little wine left in them), a crumpled napkin, and an ivory rose delicately placed stand out from the whiteness of the cloth. Each element seems suspended in time, after a prologue to an event revealed by the bag and

the sunshade left on the bench, and the hat hanging from the branch – possibly an allusion to *The Italian Straw Hat*, the comedy which had enabled Labiche to build a villa opposite La Grenouillère. The very shadow becomes light to convey the thousand vibrations in this corner of a garden with its old-fashioned charm, where a few sunrays deposit blotches on the cloth and the boy.

In contrast with the silent life of the objects and the pyschological remoteness of the people, the garden is bursting with vitality in a profusion of flowers: ranges of reds, the vermilion of the geraniums, the scarlet of the busy lizzies and the

fuchsias, the blue note of the ageratums, and the white of the soapwort. Flower beds, bouquets, flower pots, and rose trees in bloom sketch in the space of their undulating or vaporous masses. In the background the house interests the painter no more than its inhabitants. In those years 1873-1874 flowers and gardens made up an important part of his output. In that respect he was following the fashion, which for several years, had turned all Parisians into gardeners; there was not a magazine without its gardening column. But with Monet this passion was no fad. It lasted and even grew until it became almost obsessive in the *Water Lilies*.

BOULEVARD DES CAPUCINES

Monet's relations with the capital varied from one period to another. At the age of seventeen he had one sole ambition: to rediscover the city where he was born, that "astounding Paris" whose monuments and sites inspired him to paint several views. In 1867 he set up his easel in the colonnade of the Louvre, choosing an overhead perspective in the style of the masters of the Japanese print which was becoming increasingly fashionable, to depict *The Quai du Louvre*, *The Jardin de l'Infante* and *Saint-Germain-l'Auxerrois*, in which the tiny figures are still drawn with a certain precision. In 1873 the angle of sight is the same but applied now to the busiest district

BOULEVARD DES CAPUCINES, 1873
Oil on canvas, 60 x 80 cm
Pushkin Museum, Moscow

of the city. The spot has not been chosen at random. The search for a suitable venue for the future group exhibition is about to end. Nadar would lend the famous red studio which he no longer used at 35 Boulevard des Capucines. Monet placed his easel on the balcony of the second floor looking towards the Opéra Garnier, which opened two years later, and the new vaudeville theatre. The picture he undertook was a kind of signboard for one of the most fashionable boulevards and for the avant-garde exhibition which was in preparation.

In this photographers' building, occupied before Nadar by the Bissons and Le Gray, the painter adopts an overhead view, like the aerial photographs which were one of their host's many successes.

He thus did two versions, one vertical and one horizontal, of the great avenue on a fine winter's day. It is the end of December and the bare trees do not obstruct the eye; on the contrary, they form a grille through which we glimpse the crowd on the opposite pavement, the hansom cabs and landaus. The diagonal composition is ordered on two planes determined by the light: the pavement in the shade and the pavement in the sun which lights up the façades of the buildings. A host of tiny silhouettes conveyed by graphic notations swarm on the tarmac, betraying the effervescence of crowds on the eve of a holiday. The vibrations of light and the incessant hustle and bustle of the capital seem to rise up to the balcony. In the foreground on the

right two of the painter's friends are observing the boulevard, perhaps wondering how many visitors they will attract to their first exhibition. This picture was presented there and provoked the sarcasm of Leroy: "Is that what I look like when I walk along the Boulevard des Capucines? Blood and thunder! Are you making fun of me or what?" But Chesneau was delighted: "Never has the elusiveness, the fleetingness, the instantaneousness of movement been captured and fixed in its prodigious fluidity as it has in this extraordinary, marvellous sketch." For him it is not the last word in art, but a work which will echo well into the future. The interest which the 20th century has never ceased to show in Monet has proved him right.

**THE RAILWAY BRIDGE,
ARGENTEUIL,** c. 1874
Oil on canvas, 55 x 72 cm
Musée d'Orsay, Paris

**THE RAILWAY BRIDGE,
ARGENTEUIL**

In that century of
engineers, bridges and
railways were works of art,
illustrated (by Daubigny
among others) in tourist
guides and reproduced in
thousands of copies on
Choisy and Montereau
china. The presence

of a graduate of
the Polytechnique,
Henri Rouart, in the
Impressionist group may
have made Monet aware of
the aesthetic possibilities
of constructions of this
kind, in which Whistler
in London was already
interested.
His houses in Argenteuil
were both located, by
deliberate choice, near the
station where a train
arrived once an hour from
Paris-Saint-Lazare. The
subject undertaken here
has every ingredient to
seduce the painter; it is
modern and has complex
relations with the
landscape. As early
as 1870, a train from
Saint-Germain can be
seen outlined above the
meadows near Bougival
with their summer strollers
(*Train in the Country*). In a

sunnier version of this
railway bridge a sailboat
occupies center stage.
Here there is no external
element – boat, person,
dwelling – to trouble the
ephemeral encounter of
the railway and the
elements. Now that
the train is familiar (and
therefore more serene), it
no longer has the panting
breath of Turner's *Rain,
Steam and Speed*.
First and foremost it was
the imposing architecture
of the bridge – the road
bridge higher up the river
had also been the subject
of several canvases –
which interested Monet.
Its massive structure is cut
out between sky and
water, set in a vibrant
nature. It emerges from a
triangle of greenery in the
foreground: tufts of grass
held back by a fence (at

the bottom of the painter's garden), leafy branches echoed on the far bank in a more compact group. Between two piles the cross piece gives us a glimpse of the Gennevilliers bank framed as if in the lens of a camera. The land slopes gently down to the river, which is stirred by a perpetual movement. There two forces clash, two trajectories which it seems as though nothing can modify: the vertical, static one with the massive pillars, assembled in pairs like colonnades; the other is horizontal and fluid, all ripples and reflections which change with the sky, the wind, and the current. The virtual monochrome of the bridge is contrasted with the shaded swell of the river: blues and silver whites darkened with yellows and browns in the shadow of the superstructure of the bridge.

The sky, flecked with clouds – some light, some fleecy – is also a theatre for a constant movement which blends with the wisps of steam from the locomotive. The train, a major element in the picture, is barely evoked by a darker line above the parapet. Its artificial rhythm has nothing to do with the relentless flow of the Seine, the passage of the clouds or the sudden trembling of a branch. The oblique angle chosen by Monet gives an impression of speed but also of suppressed violence. However, from the clatter of its passage there will remain no more than a wisp of smoke soon blown away and the soft murmur of the dialogue of the bridge and the water.

**MADAME MONET AND HER
SON ON THE HILL,** 1875
Oil on canvas, 100 x 81 cm
*National Gallery of Art
(Mellon Collection),
Washington*

MADAME MONET AND HER
SON ON THE HILL

For some time the
contemporary world, the
goal of all Impressionist
painting, had taken on for
Monet the appearance of
his wife Camille. The first
years in Argenteuil are
filled with portraits of her.
She reads in the dazzle of
patches of sunlight, stands
at her window, amidst the
fuchsias and climbing
nasturtiums, chats beneath
the lilac, is bored with a
stranger or in a field of
daisies. Sometimes Jean is
with her, a serious little
boy minded by a maid.
This woman-flower was
soon to wither and die
and Monet is already
detaching himself
from her.
*Madame Monet and Her
Son on the Hill,* which was
hung at the second
Impressionist exhibition
in 1876, was bought in
the same year by Doctor
de Bellio. It is
impregnated with the
twofold sense of passing
time and changing
weather, like the images of
Ukiyo-e, the ephemeral,
floating world in perpetual
flux. In an admirable
layout, as light as the
woman described by
Rimbaud, "the
sunshade in her fingers
pressing the sunshade
too proud for her."

Camille is standing at the top of a hill which her son has not yet reached. Their two unequal shadows sink into the sharp green of the June grass beneath which we can make out some slight rises and falls in the ground. The small, hard, fast, stabbing touches give the foreground of the meadow a kind of motion accentuated by the range of greens barely tinged by the yellow of a few small, indecisive flowers. Longer touches swirl the clouds, which the wind seems to be shredding. It shakes the sunshade, sweeps up the skirt, blows back the veil. Monet receives those visual sensations and transmits them to the viewer. The different blues of the sky contaminate the white of the dress with their reflections. Matching the changing sky, in the eyes of the child the outfit must look like the dress of shifting colors worn by Ass's Skin.

Later Monet returned to this theme with full force, but he never rediscovered the state of grace by which this picture sums up Impressionism as a whole.

LA JAPONAISE (CAMILLE MONET IN JAPANESE COSTUME), 1875-1876
Oil on canvas,
231.6 x 142.3 cm.
Museum of Fine Arts (1951 Purchase Fund Courtesy), Boston

LA JAPONAISE (CAMILLE MONET IN JAPANESE COSTUME)

With this portrait of his wife dressed up as a Japanese woman, Monet pays a tribute which is not devoid of humor to the land of the prints which have so enriched his vision and that of so many artists of his generation. He was not the first. Whistler (*The Princess of the Land of Porcelain*, 1864), or Manet (*Portrait of Zola*, 1868, *Lady with Fans*, 1873), had made direct references to the Empire of the Rising Sun before him. There is a kind of deliberate irony in the fact of exhibiting this *Japonaise* after the Japanese allusions in *Impression, Sunrise,* with its disappointing reception. The title in the catalogue of the second Impressionist exhibition, *Japonnerie,* clearly states the painter's aim: to please with a fashionable theme and prove, as emphasized in an article by his friend Pothey (the engraver Martial) that he can "do other things than landscape." The aim is accomplished; the whole of the press is talking about the picture. Some compare *La Japonaise* to *Camille in the Green Dress* and affirm that "she blazes like a firework"; they find that she looks as if she is juggling with the fans. Others make jokes in dubious taste about the

motifs on the kimono. Monet had several; in a letter in October 1875 he says that he paints Japanese actors' costumes, which evidently refers to this picture. This Parisienne disguised as a Japanese woman seems to be a geisha straight out of a Harunobu print, represented in the same depthless arrangement. We are at the theatre, the realm of artifice, hence Camille's surprising blondness (she was a natural brunette); she seems to be laughing at her transformation. The decor consists solely of a mat with geometrical designs and "uchiwa" type fans. On the speckled blue floor and wall the fans spin around decorated with motifs in honor of that distant country: peonies, cranes, carp, mountains, figures in boats, national heroines. The viewers must also have enjoyed an allusion to contemporary politics. The Japanese lady is holding a blue, white, and red fan. "That is flattering to France," a critic noted. But also to the recently stabilized Republic, which had just definitively adopted the three colors for the flag.

Nevertheless, the true subject of the canvas is the glittering scarlet kimono with its fan-shaped train, embroidered in blue, gold, and green. The grace and lightness of the leaves and the birds in an aerial ballet are contrasted with the fury of the long-haired warrior – undoubtedly Benkei, the famous swashbuckler of Japanese literature – who is drawing his sword and rolling his enraged eyes in an opposite movement of the head to Camille's. In 1889, in his preface to the Monet-Rodin exhibition, Octave Mirbeau evoked this Japanese woman and her dress, "a miraculous country filled with the song of magical birds, gods and metamorphoses."

THE POOL AT MONTGERON, 1876
Oil on canvas, 172 x 193 cm
The Hermitage Museum,
St. Petersburg

THE POOL AT MONTGERON

Like the painter in *The Draughtsman's Contract,* Monet toured the park at Montgeron at the request of his hosts in search of viewpoints. Had he seen Constable's *Malvern Hall* in England? The façade of the mansion in the distance looks like the one in *Turkeys* and the lake in the foreground is also a mirror for the surrounding trees. However, this picture is closer to Turner's construction by "structures of color". In number one of the *Impressionniste* Georges Rivière describes the study Monet made for this canvas: "The edges of the lake with the deep, dark blue water which reflected the great trees."
The work may not have been finished at the time of the third Impressionist exhibition, although it had been undertaken the autumn before, the season when Monet was also painting autumnal scenes of the Seine at Argenteuil. The first russet leaves on the surface of the lake, the first tints of gold on the hill on the horizon where the sun still lingers. This painting, decorative

through the play of the colored values alone, expresses Monet's fascination with water. Two-thirds of the canvas are occupied by the reflection of the trees: darker on the left, under the larch; gentler on the right, perhaps beneath a lime tree. The broad horizontal touches are occasionally broken in zigzags to give the feeling of the ripples caused by the wind on the calm surface. A huge hole of light in the middle of the lake seems to sketch an immense female figure outlined like the one in *La Japonaise*.

To the right and almost invisible, a woman is fishing and her silhouette casts a shadow at her feet like the boles of the trees which frame her. Near her, at the edge of the canvas, we see a sketch of another figure. Moreover, strollers can be seen all around the lake: to the left on the boat, near the straight reflection of a trunk, in the background standing out against the bright green of the plants or emerging from beneath the trees. Diluted in the general environment, they do not even have the value of signs. Monet is already starting on the aesthetic path, which a quarter of a century later in Giverny, will open up a dialogue between the lake and the clouds from which man is excluded.

THE TURKEYS, 1876-1877
Oil on canvas,
174.5 x 172.5 cm
Musée d'Orsay, Paris

THE TURKEYS

Ernest Hoschedé must have seen the sample of decorative work provided by Monet with *The Picnic* when he commissioned him to paint four panels for his Château de Rottembourg in Montgeron in the Essonne. They represented different aspects of the park associated with the seasons: *Corner of the Garden at Montgeron*, in the spring, the rose season;

The White Turkeys, in the stifling heat of summer; *The Lake*, with the first tints of autumn; and *The Hunt*, at the onset of winter. That classical pretext did not lock the painter into a formula; he gave it a new structure, which with the canvas presented here, acquired a striking singularity. Following the example of the owner of Montgeron, Monet, so rarely an animal painter, chose these white birds for the aesthetic

interest of their blotches of light on the grass, as Anatole de Monzie would do later in the Parc de Vialolles where only animals of a spotless whiteness appeared. The different birds in Hokusai's *Manga*, unveiled some time before by Bracquemond, are not unconnected with the decorative importance of these turkeys. Moreover, their way of tackling the slope in a sinuous movement evokes certain photographs taken by the team of the Bisson brothers climbing the Alps.

Few pictures by Monet give such a feeling of tactile pleasure in the way of intersecting the touches and building with color. Here the play of reflections is not applied to a mirror or to the silky surface of a dress, but to the pale livery of these almost ghostly creatures. The scarlet of their wattled necks contrasts with their white feathers, which the setting sun lights with pink reflections while elsewhere the grass tinges them with green and the quills are shaded with blue.

Does Monet remember his days as a caricaturist when he gives the turkeys poses like elegant old ladies drawn by Rowlandson? Does he not also slip into this subject some slightly perverse allusions to the meaning of the word "dindon" (turkey) and the verb "dindonner," much in use at the time, which means to dupe someone? We may also wonder whom that eye in the foreground fixed on the viewer is staring at.

To do his painting the

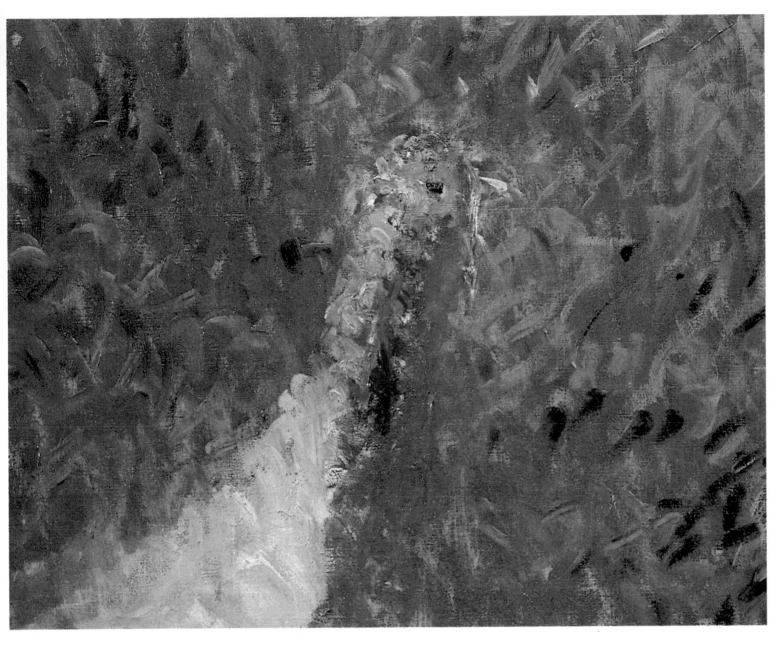

artist installed himself looking up at the meadow on the banks of the Yerres and so a seesaw movement seems to distance the perspective at the end of which we see the mansion even more. We shall find those distant pink façades charged with mystery again later in the work of Degouve de Nuncques and Magritte. That domain beneath a stormy sky does not evoke the events of the summer; it seems ready to fade away over the horizon even before a lien on the property came to tear it away from the Hoschedé family.

"*The Turkeys*, unfinished panel" – as described in the catalogue for the third Impressionist exhibition in 1877 – unleashed a chorus of mockery at the show. "That clever, deliciously executed decoration, as delicious as the most unexpected Japanese drawings, provoked hoots of laughter," Octave Mirbeau recalled in his *Notes sur l'Art*. But the work represents a peak of Monet's art, both because of its plastic splendor and because of that strangeness that seems to be a prelude to the discoveries of Surrealism.

**THE GARE
SAINT-LAZARE,** 1877
Oil on canvas, 75.5 x 104 cm
Musée d'Orsay, Paris

THE GARE SAINT-LAZARE

In the open country or in a station, in summer in the sun, in winter in the snow, Monet painted trains: a fascination for a means of transport which changed the life of a whole generation. The magic of stations, those "cathedrals of the new humanity," as Théophile Gautier called them, where the everyday and the dream stand side by side. The Gare Saint-Lazare can be seen in the work of Manet; in *Le Pont de l'Europe* Caillebotte represented figures leaning on the bridge as if they were watching Monet at work. Indeed, the painter obtained authorization to set up in the station and the immediate surroundings – the Pont de l'Europe, the Batignolles cutting, and tunnel. Feeling its secret pulse, he gave pride of place in turn to the architecture, the locomotives, the signals, and the tracks. Visions drowned in steam, perhaps inspired by Degas, who in his notebooks planned to do a "series", notably to devote one to "smoke: of locomotives, tall chimneys, factories, steamboats."

The eight canvases exhibited at the third Impressionist exhibition in 1877 did not pass unnoticed. Hostile or kind, the critics recognized their importance. The reviewer in *Le Figaro* wrote, under the pseudonym of Baron Grimm, "The artist wanted to produce the impression of a train leaving, a train about to leave, and he tried in the end to give us the disagreeable impression of

several locomotives whistling at the same time." Banville criticized this "accumulation of multicolored blotches." But Zola, the author of *The Beast in Man*, noted in the *Sémaphore de Marseille* : "You can hear the rumble of the trains pulling in, you can see smoke spilling out and rolling under the vast roof. That is where painting is today in those modern frames which are so beautifully wide. Our artists have to find the poetry of stations as their fathers found the poetry of forests and flowers." Monet did the present version in the part reserved for the local lines that went to the Impressionists' favorite spots: Chatou, Argenteuil, Vétheuil, Giverny. He lingers, rarely enough for him, over the details

of this new architecture of glass and iron which was transforming the capital. Open to the city, it reveals pink and blue buildings emerging from haze of sun and smoke. The metal framework becomes a gigantic calligraphy where the geometry of signs – the triangle of the roof and the squares of the panes of glass, the criss-cross of the rails, the line of the pillars – imposes itself through the arabesques drawn by the smoke, creating a rigorous composition based on the locomotive. It is through a similar transformation of space that Mondrian would turn towards abstraction. Monet's purposes are different: to express the dissolving power of light, to exalt the role of the machine, a dark mass blurred by the steam, to

minimize the presence of man. The crowd of passengers is reduced to little red or blue dots. An employee stands out, so fragile too in his dark work uniform. The blue and white puffs swirling beneath the glass roof or spreading out in sheets invade the space and give the station an unreal atmosphere.

With the *Windmills of Zaandam*, this vast symphony of colors and noises is another prelude to the "series" of the future, but Monet is still not representing, as he will do in the *Stacks of Wheat*, successive alterations to a single form.

THE SEINE AT VÉTHEUIL, c. 1879
Oil on canvas, 60 x 81 cm
Musée d'Orsay, Paris

THE SEINE AT VÉTHEUIL

"I have pitched my tent at Vétheuil, a delightful spot," Monet wrote to Murer in 1878. Between the Seine and the Route des Crêtes, the village provides a succession of landscapes to tempt the artist. From his youth when he took the river, like Henry James and so many travellers from Paris to Le Havre, the painter's eye must have rested on this pleasing hamlet. His critical financial situation,

his wife's illness, a child to look after, and life shared with the Hoschedés, who were now ruined, forced him to work like a slave in the immediate surroundings of his new home.

Certain motifs – sunset on the water as in *Impression, Sunrise*, fields of poppies, apple trees in blossom – return to themes he had already treated; others, such as the views of Vétheuil or Lavacourt on the opposite bank suggested new subjects, though less original than *The Flags*, the last works he had done in Paris. The deaths of Corot in 1875 and of Daubigny in 1878 left a vacuum in the life of French landscape painting. Anxious to reach a public that was still wary of the avant-garde, Monet

undertook a series of general views of Vétheuil which immediately found buyers.

Dated 1879 and exhibited in April that year at the fourth Impressionist exhibition, this canvas, which belonged to Duret at the time, is a perfect illustration of the painter's interest in all meteorological phenomena.

The sun, which has reappeared from behind the scattered clouds, bathes the new green of the slopes of Le Chênay. The Seine is still rippling from the recent rain with a shimmer reminiscent of Turner. The scene takes place in the late morning, as the line of houses is already in the full light while in the middle of the river the shadow of the willows still stretches towards the Lavacourt bank where Monet is standing in his studio-boat to fix the image.

A foreground of water of the kind Daubigny often painted and the blue line of the islets flooded by a Seine which is still running high isolate the little hamlet and hide the Romanesque tower which appears so often in his work. The only thing that counts is the effect of the sun after the rain, and Vétheuil here is just an anonymous village behind a curtain of trees.

THE FROST, 1880
Oil on canvas, 61 x 100 cm
Musée d'Orsay, Paris

THE FROST

In the winter of 1879-1880, the thermometer beat all records: −25°C in Paris in December. The Seine was frozen over; people walked on the ice between Vétheuil and Lavacourt. The snowfalls made the landscapes of Vexin look like the Scandinavia of the tales of Andersen. Monet's imagination received a healthy shock from that extraordinary spectacle which unfolded in two acts: the freeze and the thaw. The result was a number of canvases in quite different spirits. The freeze conveyed the painter's jubilation at the wintry splendor. The ones of the thaw, painted after the break up of the gigantic ice floes had crushed everything in its path, express a tragically silent beauty.

Effects of snow, of frost, ice floes drifting like huge water lilies; they all share the leitmotiv of the solidified surface of the river with its interplay between the reflections of the ice and those of the changing sky. Monet found the most beautiful effects of frost on a small backwater of the Seine between the islets. His conception of landscape had evolved considerably since *The Magpie*, where the subtlety of the harmonies of whites was applied to forms which were still affirmed. It was a more Turnerish vision of nature, more concerned with atmospheric vibrations.

The layout of this

painting, which is part of Caillebotte's legacy to the nation, is identical to that of *The Pool at Montgeron*: an empty circumference surrounded by trees which animates the play of reflections. In the foreground, a still life, in the primary meaning of the term: bushes with swords of ice hanging from the branches, a dark boat immobilized by the freeze. On either side a circle of trees, bushes and walls of vibrating scrub where the gold of an invisible sun sometimes prevails over the frosty whiteness. In the background, standing against the orange-pink sky softened with lilacs, poplars and willows sketch an aerial architecture.

The Seine occupies center stage, a silent arena where the only combats are fought between the sun and the frost. The touches of blue and pink create an iridescent surface which brings life to the winter pallor, far from the melancholy versions of the thaw which later drew so many parallels between the frozen desolation of the landscape and the recent death of Camille.

THE ROCKS OF BELLE-ÎLE, 1886
Oil on canvas, 65 x 81 cm
Musée d'Orsay, Paris

THE ROCKS OF BELLE-ÎLE

After the shores of the Mediterranean, after a brief sojourn in Holland, this visit to Belle-Île in Brittany marks Monet's third painting campaign; he was always on a quest for new motifs. The west coast, called the "Côte Sauvage," offers "a splendidly wild landscape; piles of fearful rocks and a sea of incredible colors. I was used to painting the Channel and I naturally had my routine, but the Ocean is something else," he wrote to Caillebotte. On the first days the painter was at a loss. He confided to Alice Hoschedé: "You need time to learn how to paint that." The rigorous arrangements of his earlier seascapes – the verticals of the cliffs at Pourville (1881) and Dieppe (1882), the roundness of the beaches at Étretat and Varengeville (1882), the arch of the Manneporte in Étretat (1883) – have disappeared. At Belle-Île, Monet first tries to render the eternal confrontation of sea and rock, whether he is looking at the Pyramids at Port-Coton or the Radenec rocks near the Apothicairerie Grotto. The sky, which occupies a minute part of the canvas, bounces its mauves and saffrons off an emerald sea and their two lines merge in a perfect horizontality. In the foreground the heaps of rock, carved by the resistance of granite and schist to the pounding of the waves, raise their compact forms on the slack tide. In the calm of the morning after a storm, light or dark values accentuate the contrasts between solid and liquid elements. The dark Atlantic breakers become lighter as they approach the shore; their hard undertow turns into little waves shot through with jade, sapphire, and cobalt. They dance around the islets, encircling, plunging into a hollow, exploding in a burst of silver foam. Impassive spectator of these watery manoeuvres, the rock exudes an impression of power by its volume, its dominant position, its presence as witness to a shore which has long since disappeared. As a "rustic alchemist" (in Geffroy's words), Monet attempts to render the intense life of this violet brown granite, shot through here and there with scarlet and green. He details the slightest wrinkle, digs with his brush for the tiniest irregularity, draws on his long experience: "I am well aware that in order to really paint the sea you have to see it every day, at every hour of the day and on the same spot, to discover the life of the place; I also redo the same motifs as many as four or even six times." A procedure which marks a milestone along the road to the future "series".

MEADOWS AT GIVERNY, 1888
Oil on canvas, 92 x 80 cm
*The Hermitage Museum,
St. Petersburg*

MEADOWS AT GIVERNY

Giverny is surrounded by fields and meadows. They storm up to the slopes where the village nestles, they stretch as far as the banks of the Seine, dominated on the left bank by the heights of Bonnières. Monet drew inspiration from them for works with identical themes to the ones he treated in Argenteuil and Vétheuil, though they are different in conception. The flora of the countryside seem to act as ranges of color with the hayfields in spring, the fields of poppies, the patches of daisies, and wild mustard beneath the poplars.
Here the season of flowers has passed; the grass has been mown and the effects of coloring on the immense surface of the meadow are limited to the discreet plays of light and shadow caused by the clouds passing by. This is a view of the kind one sees through a window. Pissarro had just produced a similar one in 1886 at the eighth Impressionist exhibition (*View from my Window*, Oxford, the Ashmolean Museum), done with a Divisionist technique. But in his canvases Pissarro always acknowledged the rural economy represented by a farmer's wife, a haymaker, or a laborer. Nothing of that in Monet. His landscapes are solely for excursions and

the pleasure of the eye. The touches placed like a succession of tiny waves mix greens, blues, chrome yellows, and burnt sienas to transcribe the meadows in summer. This painting was probably done in July or August on his return from a trip to London. That brief sojourn must have revived the interest he felt for Constable in 1870-1871, since some of the artist's essential works had been acquired in 1888 by the National Gallery and the Victoria and Albert Museum from the legacy of Isabel Constable. This *Meadows at Giverny* – one of the eleven Monets bought by the Russian collector Shchukin – seems to be the very expression of pure landscape. There is nonetheless a strange impression of distance between the spot where the painter is standing and the clumps of trees; elms and poplars alternating their round masses and their tapering points in front of the blue hills. The slightly murky sky is tinged with turquoise and willow-green striking minor chords with the surrounding vegetation. This curious layout with the huge void in the foreground is explained once we know that the landscape would serve as a background for Monet in two other canvases: *Landscape, Gray Light*, in which Jean Monet and Suzanne Hoschedé appear, and *Landscape with Figures, Giverny*. In this second picture, Michel Monet and Jean-Pierre Hoschedé appear in the foreground framing Germaine Hoschedé; they are cut off at the knee, while Jean and Suzanne are walking forward behind them. The use of a different touch (in a diagonal), the light scattered on the faces with no relation to the powdering of the landscape indicates that the figures were put in later. Thus the painting in the Hermitage is a precise illustration of the working method which Monet always kept so secret.

BOATING ON THE EPTE, 1887
Oil on canvas, 133 x 145 cm
Museu de Arte, São Paulo

BOATING ON THE EPTE

"I am pleased that you are doing figures in the open air. That is what we expect of you," Mirbeau wrote to Monet in 1887. The writer thus took over from the dealers, who having got Pissarro to try his hand at figures, were trying to persuade Monet not to be exclusively a landscape painter. The view of his future stepdaughters boating on the Epte aroused his interest in a type of composition that had been treated by Manet (*Argenteuil*), Renoir (*Young Girl in a Boat*), Berthe Morisot (*Summer Days*), and Caillebotte in his superb scenes of boatmen on the Yerres. He made six attempts at this scene which brings together some of the favorite elements of his artistic universe. Each time his vision is different. *Young Girls in a Boat* (Tokyo Museum) belongs to the classical form of his Impressionism: reflections of young girls (Suzanne and Blanche Hoschedé) and their boat on a sunlit stretch of water tinged with pink and blue. *Boat at Giverny* (Musée d'Orsay) is closer to one of his aims: "Figures in the open air... done like landscapes." He drew out of that use of reflections a kind of ambiguity which is verging on Symbolism. Germaine and Blanche are fishing but between them Suzanne, the prettiest of the sisters, is absorbed in the narcissistic contemplation of her

image in the water. The dense vegetation of the Île aux Orties had already invaded the picture. In the canvas shown here, it builds a wall like a Medieval green hedge behind the boat. The yellow rays of the sun enliven the blue green thickness of the leaves, where the jagged roundness contrasts with the tresses of grass under the water. Mallarmé had asked him to illustrate his prose poem *La Gloire* and Berthe Morisot to do *Nénuphar blanc*, which would have suited Monet better, and he is perhaps unconsciously referring to it in this evocation of the "sleeping vegetation" and the skiff passing rapidly by. In a letter to Geffroy in June 1890 he stresses the problems posed by this picture: "I have undertaken things which are impossible to do: water

with grasses waving in the depths... it drives you mad to want to do it." The current carries away the long grasses, sometimes swept with purple or stained with that blue that the sky allows to filter through the canopy

of branches. The pink of the dresses and the mahogany of the skiff serve as a counterpoint to the green harmony of the whole. In the diagonal composition of the bank and the boat, the oar opens an angle where the effect of speed may be perceived. With an infinitely less realistic conception, we think of the American Eakins (a friend of Walt Whitman), whose rowing scenes were familiar to all of his fellow countrymen who began to frequent Giverny. *Boating on the Epte* establishes a psychological relation between Monet and his models which is rare for him. Here the instantaneousness combines with the young girls' impatient indifference to the artist trying to capture their image. On that dark water where those snake-like grasses slither, they seem to be fleeing from the restricted circle of the family and Giverny.

STACKS OF WHEAT,
LATE SUMMER: MORNING
EFFECT, 1890
Oil on canvas, 60.5 x 100.5 cm
Musée d'Orsay, Paris

STACKS OF WHEAT, LATE
SUMMER: MORNING
EFFECT

An important stage in
Monet's work, the *Stacks*
of Wheat consecrate the
term "series", used later
for the *Poplars*, the
Cathedrals and the *Views*
of the Thames. One stack
of wheat, two stacks of
wheat, three stacks
of wheat... Like a
children's chant, Monet
counts off the stacks of
wheat through the seasons
(summer, autumn, winter),
but also through the day
and even through the
hours. He is following the
example of the masters of
the Japanese print,
Hiroshige or Hokusai, and
their famous series, among
them those of Mount Fuji.
"...I stubbornly decide on a

series of different effects,
but at this time of year the
sun goes down so quickly
that I cannot follow it...
What I am looking for:
'instantaneousness',
especially the envelope,
the same light spread
everywhere," Monet wrote
to Geffroy in October
1890. Millet, Pissarro,
Van Gogh, and many
others have represented
the theme; he had too,
in 1884, 1885, 1887.
But here his purpose is
different. In this set of a
score of pictures, it is the
intimate texture of the
stacks of wheat and their
metamorphosis with each
variation in the light that
fascinate the painter. He
tries to convey, but in his
own way, the optical
phenomena applied by
Seurat in his work and

which had become something of a fad. For that purpose, the varnished stalks of grain lend themselves admirably to the play of complementary elements. Located in the Clos Morin, to the west of his property at Giverny, they look like meteorites fallen from the sky into a nature from which all human presence is excluded. They stand alone or in pairs, close together or far apart, in an almost abstract environment. Monet roams around them, and with the shadows they throw, these stacks of wheat, a major element in any rural landscape at the time, assume an important function as sundials. The invisible sun of a "given instant" projects its early morning shadow here. Firmly anchored to the ground to resist the wind, these compact forms look more solid than the straw huts of the Universal Exhibition of 1889 evoked by their conical hats. Three parallel bands serve as backdrops, narrower for the sky, fleecier for the vegetation, more wrinkled for the stubble where the gradations of green blend with the pink. Farms, less visible than in other versions, are blurred amidst the trees. A light mist on the Seine valley indicates that summer is coming to an end. All the heat stored by the grain comes out through the warm shades: an incredible range of oranges mixed with purple, mauve, and pink, deepening on the shady parts. The only movement comes from the shadows: one encircles the base of a

stack, the other spreads out in a dark sheet. On the ground bits of straw throw bursts of blue, mauve, and orange here and there. Looking at these images of the joy of painting, Pissarro remarked: "These canvases breathe contentment." But he is surprised: "I do not know how it does not bother Monet to be tied to that repetition." Mallarmé declared that he was so "astonished" that he found himself "looking at the fields through the memory of the painting: or rather they strike me that way." The same admiration in the 20th century came from Vlaminck, Derain, and Mondrian, but most of all, Kandinsky... "What was perfectly clear to me was the unsuspected power of the palette which until then had been hidden and which went beyond all my dreams. Painting received a fabulous force and impetus from it. But, also unconsciously, the object as indispensable element of the picture was also discredited." As Kandinsky believed, through the magic of a painter, a simple stack of wheat can bring "Spirituality into Art."

ROUEN CATHEDRAL, THE PORTAL AND THE TOUR SAINT-ROMAIN, MORNING EFFECT, HARMONY IN WHITE, 1893
Oil on canvas, 106 x 73 cm
Musée d'Orsay, Paris

ROUEN CATHEDRAL, THE PORTAL AND THE TOUR SAINT-ROMAIN, MORNING EFFECT, HARMONY IN WHITE

Almost twenty years after the first Impressionist exhibition, Monet felt a desire for renewal. The extraordinarily creative atmosphere of the turn of the century was one reason, but he also felt a need to assert himself in the face of a new generation who saw him as a treasure, to be sure, but plagiarised by many and overtaken by the Symbolism of Gauguin. The series of *Cathedrals* was the dazzling demonstration of the endurance of his talent, with their layout so alien to all the rules of art. ("This damned cathedral is hard to do"). To carry out the project he had to spend two painting campaigns in Rouen (February to April 1892 and 1893) and to mount three observation posts: an apartment, a "draper's and tailor's" shop, and a novelty store. The canvases were finished in the studio in Giverny.
No effect of perspective, only the angle of sight varies slightly: the west

façade appears sometimes face on, sometimes with an opening onto the Saint-Romain Tower. Sometimes, like here, a few houses can be seen. The amount of sky tells us exactly where the painter was standing.
During those sessions, doubt, exasperation, and satisfaction alternated, as we can read in Monet's correspondence: "I am a broken man," he confided to Alice on 3 April 1892.

"I cannot take any more and I have just spent a night haunted by nightmares: the cathedral was falling on top of me, it looked blue or pink or yellow."
This façade is a face which Monet observed, scrutinized, peered, lying in wait for a bird to fly by, capturing a reflection, scanning the crumbling of the stone as Rembrandt scanned the lines on a human face. The cathedral

appears in its successive phases decked out in brown, white, gray, pink, blue, and gold harmonies. In this morning effect, some buildings and a flock of jackdaws give the scale and accentuate the effect of height of the Saint-Romain Tower, cut off in its upward thrust by the frame. This is not the Gothic architecture seen by Bonnington and Turner, but the inner life of the stone gnawed by the centuries and the inclement weather, coming to life in the rays of the morning sun which the painter attempts to show. He uses a thick texture, "variegated mortar" as Clemenceau called it, "ground onto the canvas in a fit of fury." The general harmony of the canvas, a cameo of blue and mauve, is enhanced with pink and white. Some parts seem to be dislocated by the effect of a golden light; others, such as the ochre porch or the rose window encased in blue and pink, stand out from the whole.
Twenty versions presented at Durand-Ruel's gallery in 1894 were hailed by artists (Pissarro, Cézanne, Signac) and critics as an event. A discovery of "a new way of looking, of feeling, of expressing a revolution," Clemenceau wrote in an article with the resounding title *La Révolution des "Cathédrales"*.
After them, in the 20th century Picasso, Braque, and Roy Lichtenstein, to name but a few, agree with Malevich in attributing to these façades "a capital importance in the history of art" which obliged "whole generations to change their conceptions."

LONDON, HOUSES OF PARLIAMENT, SUN THROUGH THE FOG, 1904
Oil on canvas, 81 x 92 cm
Musée d'Orsay, Paris

LONDON, HOUSES OF PARLIAMENT, SUN THROUGH THE FOG

"I would like to try to paint some effects of fog on the Thames." That phrase of Monet's accompanied the announcement of a journey to London in late 1887. It had taken him twelve years to get the project off the ground and four more to complete it. Fog on the harbor at Le Havre, on the Seine at Vétheuil, on the poplars by the Epte. Monet had always surpassed himself at each stage of his career in the standard subjects of Impressionism. Moreover, he had a permanent need to measure himself against certain masters. With *The Picnic* he had confronted Manet. With the views of the Thames, Turner and Whistler were the objects of his wish for emulation. Their exhibitions at Petit's gallery and a reciprocal admiration brought him close to Whistler, who with Sargent, encouraged him to come to London. "To be free of any spirit of imitation... to create shades." That example which with Signac was inspired by Turner in 1898 is of the same order as the step Monet took.

He began his first tests at the Savoy Hotel in the autumn of 1899 and returned in February. Maupassant had observed him at Étretat, accompanied by children carrying canvases on which he jotted his successive impressions. In London that system of work reached the point of frenzy. Fifty pictures were already begun on 11 March 1900, and eighty at the end of the same month. "How difficult to render this variable atmosphere." From his room he did the views of the bridges (Charing Cross and Waterloo), but it was on the opposite bank that he set up his easel for the Houses of Parliament series. A friend of Sargent's, Mrs Hunter, had obtained him authorization to paint each afternoon in a room on the terrace of St. Thomas's Hospital opposite the building. Turner had painted the fire at the old Houses of Parliament, Monet showed the new houses in the flames of the sunset. Here the sun is trying to break through the thick fog of industrial

civilization. The canvas is bathed in a crimson violet. He seems to be projecting the favorite color of Queen Victoria, whose funeral was held during the artist's last painting campaign in London. This picture, like the others, was finished in Giverny after some trying work sessions comparing the different versions. Quite different from Whistler's *Westminster, Nocturne in Gray and Gold*, as light as a puff of air, this Parliament is ghostlike in the manner of the "burgs" of Victor Hugo, a relative of his Lecadre cousins through the Vacqueries. But the work does not dissociate itself from the currents of its time through the exaggeration of color. A cobalt blue is applied to all the zones of shadow, a scarlet mixed with vermilion to the reflection of the sun, which turns the Thames into a river of blood. Impressionist, to be sure, in the almost woven touches, this picture is a prelude to Fauvism by its simplifications and that expressiveness of color which Derain was to take up the following year for his own series of *The Thames*. When they were exhibited in 1904, Monet's London canvases inspired the lyricism of Mirbeau and all his friends and undoubtedly drew the attention of Apollinaire, whose *Song of the Ill-beloved* whispers: "An evening of light mist in London."

BLUE WATER LILIES

A garden encloses, cuts off, consoles. At the end of his life Monet never went far away. Since he conceived his water garden, that magic mirror of summer gradually became "his sole motif, represented," he said, "in all its happenings." The rather easy theme of the slender bridge (inspired by the "marvellous views of famous bridges by Hokusai") gradually vanished from his pictures and gave way to the *Water Lilies*, a series of water landscapes exhibited in 1909 at Durand-Ruel's gallery. Proust took from them his admirable description of the lilies on the Vivonne. The plant had fascinated the poets Monet had read. "The great water lilies on the calm waters," sang Verlaine. And Mallarmé saw them "enveloping in their hollow whiteness a nothing made of untouched dreams." They were also one of the favorite motifs of the Modern Style. Gallé and Georges de Feure decorated vases, candelabras, and fabrics with them. Monet himself was turning towards this interpretation in his project for the "Great Decorations" which he had envisaged earlier and returned to in 1915. It was from them that Clemenceau came on 18 November 1918 to

BLUE WATER-LILIES,
1916-1919
Oil on canvas, 200 x 200 cm
Musée d'Orsay, Paris

choose the two canvases that the painter wanted to offer the nation in honor of the armistice. That was when he persuaded him to paint the great set which is in the Orangerie today. Unnoticed by the Cubists, the plastic qualities of the *Water Lilies* found an echo in the Surrealists and were a prelude, as Jean-Dominique Rey has shown, to lyrical abstraction. The owner of these *Blue Water Lilies* before they entered the Musée d'Orsay was Tériade, the director of one of the most interesting art magazines, *Verve*. They compose a variation on circular forms: the branches and their reflections sketch a circle inside which the rounded leaves and pink-tinged cups of the water lilies – "a light-temptation-pink" as Bachelard said, "without which the white would never be aware of its whiteness" – overlap. Only the branches of the willows planted on the north bank of the pond can be seen. They undulate on the blue surface like Mélisande's hair, an association of images which Monet, an admirer of Maeterlinck and Debussy, was probably unconsciously projecting. The *Water Lilies* represent the final break with the traditional landscape of Corot or Daubigny. They are also in the straight line of an investigation devoted to all the subtleties of perception and which, in the year of the picture, led Gourmont to declare that "Impressionism is Monet himself, isolated in his genius, a glorious miracle worker."

MONET

THE COMPLETE WORKS

WORKS

1 • Still Life with Pheasant, 1861
Oil on canvas, 76 x 62 cm
Musée des Beaux-Arts, Rouen

2 • Corner of a Studio, 1861
Oil on canvas, 182 x 127 cm
Musée d'Orsay, Paris

3 • Hunting Trophy, 1862
Oil on canvas, 104 x 75 cm
Musée d'Orsay, Paris

4 • Farmyard in Normandy, c. 1863
Oil on canvas, 65 x 81.3 cm
Musée d'Orsay, Paris

5 • Beach with Small Boats Near Honfleur, 1864
Oil on canvas, 57 x 81 cm
Private Collection

6 • The Pointe de la Hève, 1864
Oil on canvas, 41 x 73 cm
Private Collection

7 • The Hospice Lighthouse, 1864
Oil on canvas, 54 x 81 cm
Jöhr Collection, Zurich

8 • Still Life with Meat, c. 1864
Oil on canvas, 24 x 33 cm
Musée d'Orsay, Paris

9 • The Mouth of the Seine at Honfleur, 1865
Oil on canvas, 90 x 150 cm
Private Collection

10 • The Picnic, 1865
Oil on canvas, 130 x 181 cm
Pushkin Museum, Moscow

11 • The Strollers (Bazille and Camille), 1865
Oil on canvas, 94 x 69 cm
National Gallery of Art, Washington

12

13 14

15 16

17 18

19 20

21 22

**12 • Le pavé de Chailly
(The Road of Chailly), c. 1865**
Oil on canvas, 43.5 x 59 cm
Musée d'Orsay, Paris

13 • The Picnic, 1865-1866
Oil on canvas (fragment), 418 x 150 cm
Musée d'Orsay, Paris

14 • The Picnic, 1865-1866
Oil on canvas,
(central part) 248 x 217 cm
Musée d'Orsay, Paris

15 • Camille or The Green Dress, 1866
Oil on canvas, 231 x 151 cm
Kunsthalle, Bremen

16 • Camille with a Dog, 1866
Oil on canvas, 73 x 54 cm
Private Collection

17 • Garden in Bloom, c. 1866
Oil on canvas, 65 x 54 cm
Musée d'Orsay, Paris

**18 • Rue de la Bavolle at Honfleur,
c. 1866 (?)**
Oil on canvas, 56 x 61 cm
Museum of Fine Arts, Boston

**19 • Women in the Garden,
1866-1867**
Oil on canvas, 255 x 205 cm
Musée d'Orsay, Paris

**20 • Garden at Sainte-Adresse
or The Terrace at Sainte-Adresse,
1866-1867**
Oil on canvas, 98 x 130 cm
*The Metropolitan Museum of Art,
New York*

21 • The Jardin de l'infante, 1867
Oil on canvas, 91 x 62 cm
Allen Memorial Art Museum, Oberlin

22 • The Quai du Louvre, 1867
Oil on canvas, 65 x 92 cm
Haags Gemeentemuseum, The Hague

WORKS

23 • The Beach at Sainte-Adresse, 1867
Oil on canvas, 75 x 101 cm
The Art Institute, Chicago

24 • The Road to the Saint-Siméon Farm, 1867
Oil on canvas, 56 x 81 cm
The Fogg Art Museum, Cambridge (Massachusetts)

25 • Still Life with Pears and Grape, 1867
Oil on canvas, 46 x 56 cm
Astor Collection, New York

26 • Jeanne-Marguerite Lecadre in the Garden, 1867
Oil on canvas, 80 x 99 cm
The Hermitage Museum, St. Petersburg

27 • Saint-Germain-l'Auxerrois, 1867
Oil on canvas, 79 x 98 cm
Nationalgalerie, Staatliche Museen, Berlin

28 • Regattas at Sainte-Adresse, c. 1867
Oil on canvas, 75.3 x 101 cm
The Metropolitan Museum of Art, New York

29 • Cart, Road Under Snow, Near Honfleur, c. 1867
Oil on canvas, 65 x 92.5 cm
Musée d'Orsay, Paris

30 • Near Honfleur. Snow, c. 1867
Oil on canvas, 81.5 x 102 cm
Musée du Louvre, Paris

31 • The Jetty at Le Havre in Bad Weather, 1867-1868
Oil on canvas, 51.5 x 61 cm
Gabriel Sabet Collection, Genève

32 • Boats on the Sea, 1868
Oil on canvas, 96 x 130 cm
The Hill-Stead Museum, Farmington

33 • Madame Gaudibert, 1868
Oil on canvas, 217 x 138.5 cm
Musée d'Orsay, Paris

23

24

25

26

27

28

29

30

31

32

33

34   35   36

37   38

39   40

41   42

43   44

34 • Luncheon, 1868
Oil on canvas, 230 x 150 cm
*Städelsches Kunstinstitut und
Städtische Galerie, Frankfurt*

**35 • On the Bank of the River,
Bennecourt, 1868**
Oil on canvas, 81 x 100 cm
The Art Institute, Chicago

36 • The Dinner, 1868
Oil on canvas, 52 x 65 cm
Bührle Collection, Zurich

37 • Interior after Dinner, 1868
Oil on canvas, 50 x 65 cm
National Galllery of Art, Washington

**38 • Rough Sea at Étretat,
1868-1869**
Oil on canvas, 66 x 131 cm
Musée d'Orsay, Paris

**39 • Portrait of J. F. Jacquemart
with an Umbrella, 1868-1869**
Oil on canvas, 100 x 61 cm
Kunsthaus, Zurich

40 • The Magpie, 1869
Oil on canvas, 89 x 130 cm
Musée d'Orsay, Paris

41 • La Grenouillère, 1869
Oil on canvas, 74.6 x 99.7 cm
*The Metropolitan Museum of Art,
New York*

42 • Red Fish, 1869
Oil on canvas, 36 x 50 cm
*The Fogg Art Museum, Cambridge
(Massachusetts)*

**43 • The Bridge at Bougival,
1869-1870**
Oil on canvas, 63.5 x 91.5 cm
*Currier Gallery of Art, Manchester
(New Hampshire)*

44 • The Beach at Trouville, 1870
Oil on canvas, 54 x 65 cm
Wadsworth Atheneum, Hartford

WORKS

45 • The Beach at Trouville, 1870
Oil on canvas, 48 x 74 cm
Private Collection

**46 • The Hôtel des Roches-Noires,
Trouville, 1870**
Oil on canvas, 80 x 58.5 cm
Musée d'Orsay, Paris

47 • The Beach at Trouville, 1870
Oil on canvas, 38 x 46 cm
The National Gallery, London

48 • On the Beach, Trouville, 1870
Oil on canvas, 38 x 46 cm
Musée Marmottan, Paris

49 • Camille on the Beach, 1870
Oil on canvas, 30 x 15 cm
Musée Marmottan, Paris

**50 • Ice-floes on the Seine at
Bougival, 1869-1870**
Oil on canvas, 65 x 81.2 cm
Musée du Louvre, Paris

**51 • The Red Hood
(Madame Monet), 1870**
Oil on canvas, 100 x 80 cm
The Museum of Art, Cleveland

**52 • Road in Louveciennes
(Snow Effect), 1870**
Oil on canvas, 55 x 65 cm
Nelson-Harris Collection

**53 • Meditation. Madame Monet
on a Divan, c. 1870-1871**
Oil on canvas, 48 x 75 cm
Musée d'Orsay, Paris

**54 • Train in the Country,
c. 1870-1871**
Oil on canvas, 50 x 65 cm
Musée d'Orsay, Paris

**55 • Thames and Houses
of Parliament, 1871**
Oil on canvas, 47 x 73 cm
The National Gallery, London

45

46

47

48

49

50

51

52

53

54

55

56

57

58

59

60

61

62

63

64

65

66

56 • Hyde Park, 1871
Oil on canvas
*Museum of Art, Rhode Island School
of Design, Providence*

57 • Zaandam, 1871
Oil on canvas, 48 x 73 cm
Musée d'Orsay, Paris

**58 • Houses on the Banks
of the Zaan, at Zaandam, 1871**
Oil on canvas, 47 x 74 cm
*Städelsches Kunstinstitut und
Städtische Galerie, Frankfurt*

59 • The Voorzan, 1871
Oil on canvas, 39 x 71 cm
Private Collection

60 • Green Park, c. 1871
Oil on canvas, 34 x 72 cm
The Museum of Art, Philadelphia

61 • The Zaan at Zaandam, 1871
Oil on canvas, 42 x 73 cm
Acquavella Galleries

62 • Boats at the Zaan, 1871
Oil on canvas, 35 x 71 cm
Private Collection

63 • Windmills in Holland, 1871
Oil on canvas, 46 x 71 cm
Björkman Collection, New York

64 • Windmills Near Zaandam, 1871
Oil on canvas, 40 x 72 cm
The Walters Art Gallery, Baltimore

65 • Ships, 1871
Oil on canvas, 34 x 74 cm
Nationalmuseum, Stockholm

**66 • Portrait of Gurtjie van
de Stadt, 1871**
Oil on canvas, 73 x 40 cm
Private Collection

WORKS

67 • Windmills Near Zaandam, 1871
Oil on canvas, 47 x 73 cm
Private Collection

68 • Windmill at Zaandam, 1871
Oil on canvas, 48 x 73 cm
Private Collection

69 • Anchored ship, c. 1871-1872
Oil on canvas, 48 x 75 cm
Musée d'Orsay, Paris

70 • Impression, Sunrise, 1872
Oil on canvas, 48 x 63 cm
Musée Marmottan, Paris

71 • The Pont-Neuf,
Paris, 1871-1872 (?)
Oil on canvas, 53.5 x 73.5 cm
Museum of Art, Dallas

72 • Jean Monet on His Mechanical
Horse, 1872
Oil on canvas, 73 x 59 cm
Cummings Collection, Chicago

73 • The Stream at Robec, 1872
Oil on canvas, 65 x 65 cm
Musée d'Orsay, Paris

74 • Carrières-Saint-Denis, 1872
Oil on canvas, 61 x 81 cm
Musée d'Orsay, Paris

75 • Landscape. View of the Plain
of Argenteuil, 1872
Oil on canvas, 55 x 72 cm
Musée d'Orsay, Paris

76 • The Promenade
at Argenteuil, 1872
Oil on canvas, 50 x 65 cm
National Gallery of Art, Washington

77 • The Seine at Argenteuil, 1872
Oil on canvas, 50 x 61 cm
Musée d'Orsay, Paris

67

68

69

70

71

72

73

74

75

76

77

78

79

80

81

82

83

84

85

86

87

88

78 • Regattas at Argenteuil, 1872
Oil on canvas, 48 x 75 cm
Musée d'Orsay, Paris

79 • Argenteuil, 1872
Oil on canvas, 50 x 65 cm
Musée d'Orsay, Paris

80 • Pleasure Boats, 1872
Oil on canvas, 47 x 65 cm
Musée d'Orsay, Paris

81 • Lilacs in the Sun, 1872
Oil on canvas, 50 x 65 cm
Pushkin Museum, Moscow

**82 • The Bridge Under Repair,
Argenteuil, 1872**
Oil on canvas, 60 x 80.5 cm
Fitzwilliam Museum, Cambridge

83 • The Seine at Rouen, 1872
Oil on canvas, 50 x 78 cm
Private Collection

84 • The Pool at Argenteuil, 1872
Oil on canvas, 60 x 80.5 cm
Musée d'Orsay, Paris

85 • Still Life with Melon, 1872
Oil on canvas, 53 x 73 cm
*Calouste Gulbenkian Foundation,
Lisbon*

86 • The Wooden Bridge, 1872
Oil on canvas, 54 x 73 cm
Private Collection

87 • Tea Service, c. 1872
Oil on canvas, 52 x 72 cm
Museum of Arts (on loan), Dallas

**88 • Lilacs, Dull Weather or Repose
Beneath the Lilacs, c. 1872-1873**
Oil on canvas, 50 x 65.7 cm
Musée d'Orsay, Paris

WORKS

89 • Pleasure Boats, Argenteuil, c. 1872-1873
Oil on canvas, 49 x 65 cm
Musée d'Orsay, Paris

90 • Camille Reading, 1872-1874 (?)
Oil on canvas, 50 x 65 cm
The Walters Art Gallery, Baltimore

91 • Luncheon, 1873-1874
Oil on canvas, 160 x 201 cm
Musée d'Orsay, Paris

92 • Boulevard des Capucines, 1873
Oil on canvas, 60 x 80 cm
Pushkin Museum, Moscow

93 • Boulevard des Capucines, 1873
Oil on canvas, 80 x 60 cm
Nelson Atkins Museum of Art, Kansas City

94 • Apple Trees in Bloom, 1873
Oil on canvas, 60 x 100 cm
The Metropolitan Museum of Art, New York

95 • Apple Trees in Bloom, 1873
Oil on canvas, 61 x 100 cm
Private Collection

96 • Monet's Garden at Argenteuil (The Dahlias), 1873
Oil on canvas, 61 x 82 cm
Levin Collection

97 • Camille Monet at the Window, 1873
Oil on canvas, 60 x 49 cm
National Gallery of Art, Washington

98 • Camille in the Garden, with Jean and His Nursemaid, 1873
Oil on canvas, 59 x 79 cm
Bührle Collection, Zurich

99 • Poppies at Argenteuil, 1873
Oil on canvas, 50 x 65 cm
Musée d'Orsay, Paris

89

90

91

92

93

94

95

96

97

98

99

100

101

102

103

104

105

106

107

108

109

110

100 • Autumn Effect, Argenteuil, 1873
Oil on canvas, 56 x 75 cm
Courtauld Institute Galleries, London

101 • The Thaw, 1873
Oil on canvas, 55 x 73 cm
Private Collection

102 • The Seine at Asnières, c. 1873
Oil on canvas, 55 x 74 cm
Private Collection

103 • The Geldersekade at Amsterdam, Winter, 1874
Oil on canvas, 55 x 65 cm
Private Collection

104 • The Windmill of Onbekende Gracht, 1874
Oil on canvas, 56 x 65 cm
Private Collection

105 • The Studio-Boat, 1874
Oil on canvas, 50 x 64 cm
Rijksmuseum Kröller-Müller, Otterlo

106 • The Small Lake at Argenteuil, 1874
Oil on canvas, 55 x 73 cm
Private Collection

107 • Sailing Ship at Petit-Gennevilliers, 1874
Oil on canvas, 56 x 74 cm
Simons Collection

108 • The Railway Bridge, Argenteuil, 1874
Oil on canvas, 14 x 23 cm
Musée Marmottan, Paris

109 • The Road Bridge, Argenteuil, 1874
Oil on canvas, 60 x 80 cm
Musée d'Orsay, Paris

110 • The Railway Bridge, Argenteuil, c. 1874
Oil on canvas, 55 x 72 cm
Musée d'Orsay, Paris

WORKS

111 • The Road Bridge, Argenteuil, 1874
Oil on canvas, 60 x 80 cm
National Gallery of Art, Washington

112 • The Seine at Argenteuil, 1874
Oil on canvas, 55 x 76 cm
Private Collection

113 • The Road Bridge, Argenteuil, 1874
Oil on canvas, 54 x 73 cm
Private Collection

114 • The Road Bridge, Argenteuil, 1874
Oil on canvas, 58 x 80 cm
Bayerische Staatsgemäldesammlungen, Neue Pinakothek, Munich

115 • The Small Lake at Argenteuil, 1874
Oil on canvas, 54 x 73 cm
Museum of Art, Rhode Island School of Design, Providence

116 • Meadow at Bezons, 1874
Oil on canvas, 57 x 80 cm
Nationalgalerie, Staatliche Museen, Berlin

117 • On the Banks of the Water, Argenteuil (The Boatman's House), 1874
Oil on canvas, 55 x 65 cm
(destroyed)

118 • The Hague. Fishing Boats Leaving the Port, 1874
Oil on canvas, 60 x 101 cm
Private Collection

119 • Snow at Argenteuil, 1874
Oil on canvas, 57 x 74 cm
Museum of Fine Arts, Boston

120 • Woman Seated on a Bench (At the Park), 1874
Oil on canvas, 74 x 58 cm
The Tate Gallery, London

121 • Canal in Amsterdam, 1874
Oil on canvas, 55 x 65 cm
Comte d'Arschott Collection, Belgium

111

112

113

114

115

116

117

118

119

120

121

122

123

124

125

126

127

128

129

130

131

132

122 • View of Montalbaan's Tower, Amsterdam, 1874
Oil on canvas, 60 x 81 cm
Private Collection

123 • Boatmen at Argenteuil, c. 1874
Oil on canvas, 59 x 79 cm
Private Collection

124 • Regattas at Argenteuil, c. 1874
Oil on canvas, 60 x 100 cm
Musée d'Orsay, Paris

125 • Madame Monet and Her Son on the Hill, 1875
Oil on canvas, 100 x 81 cm
National Gallery of Art, Washington

126 • Snow Effect, Sunset, 1875
Oil on canvas, 53 x 64 cm
Musée Marmottan, Paris

127 • Snow at Argenteuil, 1875
Oil on canvas, 55 x 65 cm
National Museum of Western Art, Tokyo

128 • The Boulevard de Pontoise at Argenteuil, 1875
Oil on canvas, 60.5 x 81.5 cm
Kunstmuseum, Basel

129 • The Train in the Snow, 1875
Oil on canvas, 59 x 78 cm
Musée Marmottan, Paris

130 • Camille and Jean Monet in the House at Argenteuil, called Corner of an Apartment, 1875
Oil on canvas, 81.5 x 60.5 cm
Musée d'Orsay, Paris

131 • Poplars, Near Argenteuil, 1875
Oil on canvas, 54 x 73 cm
Haupt Collection, Palm Springs

132 • Camille Monet and a Child in the Garden, 1875
Oil on canvas, 55 x 66 cm
Webster Collection, Boston

WORKS

133 • The Monet Family in the Garden, 1875
Oil on canvas, 61 x 80 cm
Private Collection

134 • Women among the Dahlias, 1875
Oil on canvas, 54 x 65 cm
Národni Galeri, Prague

135 • Red Boats, 1875
Oil on canvas, 60 x 81 cm
The Fogg Art Museum, Cambridge (Massachusetts)

136 • Red Boats, Argenteuil, 1875
Oil on canvas, 55 x 65 cm
Musée d'Orsay, Paris

137 • The Road to Epinay, with the Effect of Snow (Road at Argenteuil), 1875
Oil on canvas, 60 x 105 cm
Albright-Knox Art Gallery, Buffalo

138 • Summer, Poppy Field, 1875
Oil on canvas, 60 x 81 cm
Trüssel Collection, Switzerland

139 • Winter Effect, Argenteuil, 1875
Oil on canvas, 61 x 82.5 cm
Private Collection

140 • Men Unloading Coal, c. 1875
Oil on canvas, 55 x 66 cm
Private Collection

141 • The Banks of the Lake at Petit-Gennevilliers, at Dusk, c. 1875
Oil on canvas, 55 x 74 cm
Formerly Gould Collection, Florence

142 • La Japonaise (Camille Monet in Japanese Costume), 1875-1876
Oil on canvas, 231.6 x 142.3 cm
Museum of Fine Arts, Boston

133

134

135

136

137

138

139

140

141

142

143

144

145

146

147

148

149

150

151

152

143 • The Gladioli, 1876
Oil on canvas, 60 x 81 cm
The Institute of Arts, Detroit

**144 • Round-Topped Tree,
Argenteuil, 1876**
Oil on canvas, 60 x 81 cm
Private Collection

**145 • Camille in the Garden,
Argenteuil, 1876**
Oil on canvas, 81 x 59 cm
*Formerly Walter H. Annenberg
Collection, Philadelphia*

**146 • Monet's House
in Argenteuil, 1876**
Oil on canvas, 63 x 52 cm
Count of Inchcape Collection, London

147 • In the Meadow, 1876
Oil on canvas, 60 x 82 cm
Private Collection

**148 • The Hunt (Avenue du Park,
Montgeron), 1876**
Oil on canvas, 137 x 170 cm
Durand-Ruel Collection, Paris

149 • Monceau Park, 1876
Oil on canvas, 60 x 81 cm
*The Metropolitan Museum of Art,
New York*

**150 • Corner of the Garden
at Montgeron, 1876**
Oil on canvas, 172 x 193 cm
Private Collection

151 • The Pool at Montgeron, 1876
Oil on canvas, 172 x 193 cm
*The Hermitage Museum,
St. Petersburg*

152 • The Tuileries, Study, c. 1876
Oil on canvas, 50 x 75 cm
Musée d'Orsay, Paris

WORKS

153 • The Tuileries, c. 1876
Oil on canvas, 54 x 73 cm
Musée Marmottan, Paris

154 • The Turkeys, 1876-1877
Oil on canvas, 174.5 x 172.5 cm
Musée d'Orsay, Paris

**155 • Corner of the Garden
at Montgeron, 1876-1877**
Oil on canvas, 173 x 193 cm
*The Hermitage Museum, St.
Petersburg*

156 • The Gare Saint-Lazare, 1877
Oil on canvas, 75 x 104 cm
Musée d'Orsay, Paris

**157 • The Gare Saint-Lazare,
the Arrival of a Train, 1877**
Oil on canvas, 82 x 101 cm
*The Fogg Art Museum, Cambridge
(Massachusetts)*

158 • The Gare Saint-Lazare, 1877
Oil on canvas, 54 x 72 cm
McLaren Collection, London

**159 • The Gare Saint-Lazare:
The Train for Normandy, 1877**
Oil on canvas, 60 x 80 cm
The Art Institute, Chicago

**160 • The Pont de l'Europe,
the Gare Saint-Lazare, 1877**
Oil on canvas, 64 x 81 cm
Musée Marmottan, Paris

**161 • Exterior of the
Gare Saint-Lazare.
Impression of Sun, 1877**
Oil on canvas, 60 x 80 cm
Private Collection

**162 • Exterior View of the
Gare Saint-Lazare, Sketch, 1877**
Oil on canvas, 65 x 81 cm
Private Collection

153

154

155

156

157

158

159

160

161

162

163

164

165

166

167

168

169

170

171

172

163 • Argenteuil, the Bank in Flower, 1877
Oil on canvas, 54 x 65 cm
Private Collection

164 • Springtime on the Island of Grande-Jatte, 1878
Oil on canvas, 50 x 61 cm
Nasjonalgalleriet, Oslo

165 • Apple Trees on the Chantemesle Coast, 1878
Oil on canvas, 64 x 81 cm
Private Collection

166 • Springtime Seen through the Branches, 1878
Oil on canvas, 52 x 63 cm
Musée Marmottan, Paris

167 • On the Banks of the Seine, Island La Grande-Jatte, 1878
Oil on canvas, 53 x 64 cm
Durand-Ruel Collection, Paris

168 • Island of La Grande-Jatte, 1878
Oil on canvas, 56 x 74 cm
Private Collection

169 • Chrysanthemums, 1878
Oil on canvas, 54 x 65 cm
Musée d'Orsay, Paris

170 • Monceau Park, 1878
Oil on canvas, 73 x 55 cm
The Metropolitan Museum of Art, New York

171 • The Rue Saint-Denis, 1878
Oil on canvas, 76 x 52 cm
Musée des Beaux Arts, Rouen

172 • Lavacourt, 1878
Oil on canvas, 60 x 90 cm
Findlay Art Galleries, New York

WORKS

173 • Portrait of Jean-Pierre Hoschedé, called « Bébé Jean », 1878
Oil on canvas, 41 x 33 cm
Formerly Gould Collection, Florence

174 • The Bank of the River, Lavacourt, 1878
Oil on canvas, 65 x 80 cm
Gemäldegalerie, Staatliche Kunstsammlungen, Dresden

175 • Apple Trees, Vétheuil, 1878
Oil on canvas, 55 x 66 cm
Dixon Collection

176 • The Road in Vétheuil, 1878
Oil on canvas, 49 x 61 cm
Arthur Murray Collection, Hawaï

177 • The Rue Montorgueil, 1878
Oil on canvas, 80 x 50.5 cm
Private Collection

178 • The Church at Vétheuil, Snow, 1878-1879
Oil on canvas, 52 x 71 cm
Musée d'Orsay, Paris

179 • The Church at Vétheuil (Winter), 1878-1879
Oil on canvas, 52 x 71 cm
Musée d'Orsay, Paris

180 • Poppy Field Near Vétheuil, 1879
Oil on canvas, 70 x 90 cm
Bührle Collection, Zurich

181 • Entrance of the Village of Vétheuil, in Winter, 1879
Oil on canvas, 60 x 81 cm
Museum of Fine Arts, Boston

182 • The Road in Vétheuil, Snow Effect, 1879
Oil on canvas, 61 x 81 cm
Private Collection

173

174

175

176

177

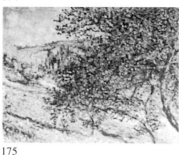

178

179

180

181

182

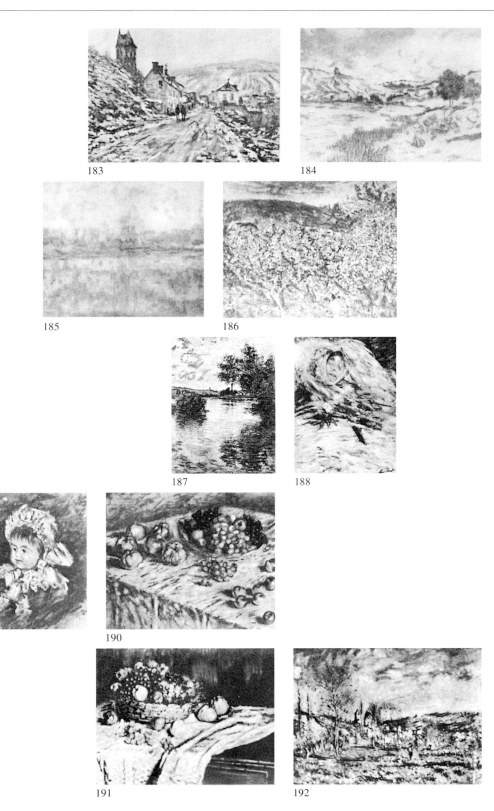

183

184

185

186

187

188

189

190

191

192

183 • The Road in Vétheuil, Winter, 1879
Oil on canvas, 53 x 72 cm
Konstmuseum, Göteborg

184 • Landscape, Vétheuil, 1879
Oil on canvas, 60 x 73 cm
Musée d'Orsay, Paris

185 • Vétheuil in the Mist, 1879
Oil on canvas, 60 x 71 cm
Musée Marmottan, Paris

186 • Plum Trees in Flower, 1879
Oil on canvas, 73 x 94 cm
Reader's Digest Collection

187 • The Seine at Vétheuil, 1879
Oil on canvas, 80 x 60 cm
Musée des Beaux-Arts, Rouen

188 • Camille Monet on Her Deathbed, 1879
Oil on canvas, 90 x 68 cm
Musée d'Orsay, Paris

189 • Portrait of Michel Monet, 1879
Oil on canvas, 46 x 37 cm
Musée Marmottan, Paris

190 • Still Life: Apples and Grapes, 1879
Oil on canvas, 65 x 82 cm
The Art Institute, Chicago

191 • Fruit Basket (Apples and Grapes), 1879
Oil on canvas, 68 x 90 cm
The Metropolitan Museum of Art, New York

192 • View of Vétheuil, Winter, 1879
Oil on canvas, 60 x 87 cm
Durand-Ruel Collection, Paris

WORKS

193 • Vase with Nasturtiums, 1879
Oil on canvas, 62 x 77 cm
Parke-Bernet Collection, New York

**194 • Lavacourt, Sun and Snow,
1879-1880**
Oil on canvas, 59 x 81 cm
The National Gallery, London

**195 • Still Life: Pheasants
and Plovers, 1879**
Oil on canvas, 68 x 90 cm
Private Collection

196 • The River at Lavacourt, 1879
Oil on canvas, 54 x 65 cm
The Art Museum, Portland

197 • The Seine at Vétheuil, c. 1879
Oil on canvas, 60 x 81 cm
Musée d' Orsay, Paris

198 • The Seine at Vétheuil, c. 1879
Oil on canvas, 43.5 x 70.5 cm
Musée d'Orsay, Paris

**199 • Snow-Covered Landscape
at Dusk, 1879-1880**
Oil on canvas, 55 x 81 cm
Musée des Beaux-Arts, Le Havre

**200 • The Seine at Vétheuil,
c. 1879-1882**
Oil on canvas, 43.5 x 70.5 cm
Musée d'Orsay, Paris

**201 • Vétheuil Seen from
Île Saint-Martin, 1880**
Oil on canvas, 65 x 81 cm
Private Collection

**202 • Portrait of Michel Monet with
Pom-Pomed Hat, 1880**
Oil on canvas, 46 x 38 cm
Musée Marmottan, Paris

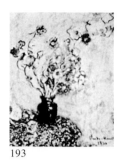
193

194

195

196

197

198

199

200

201

202

203
204

205
206
207

208
209

210

211
212

203 • Portrait of Jean Monet, 1880
Oil on canvas, 46 x 37 cm
Musée Marmottan, Paris

204 • Pears and Grape, 1880
Oil on canvas, 81 x 65 cm
Kunsthalle, Hamburg

205 • Woman Seated Under Willows, 1880
Oil on canvas, 81 x 60 cm
National Gallery of Art, Washington

206 • The Road to Roche-Guyon, 1880
Oil on canvas, 60 x 73 cm
National Museum of Western Art, Tokyo

207 • Poppy Field Near Vétheuil, 1880
Oil on canvas, 73 x 60 cm
Bührle Collection, Zurich

208 • Flowers on the Banks of the Seine Near Vétheuil, 1880
Oil on canvas, 65 x 81 cm
The Metropolitan Museum of Art, New York

209 • On the Banks of the Seine Near Vétheuil, 1880
Oil on canvas, 73 x 100 cm
National Gallery of Art, Washington

210 • The Seine at Vétheuil, 1880
Oil on canvas, 60 x 105 cm
The Metropolitan Museum of Art, New York

211 • Vétheuil in Summer, 1880
Oil on canvas, 66 x 79.7 cm
The Metropolitan Museum of Art, New York

212 • Vétheuil, 1880
Oil on canvas, 60 x 80 cm
Krupp Collection, Germany

WORKS

213 • Portrait of André Lauvray, 1880
Oil on canvas, 46 x 38 cm
Private Collection

214 • Thaw, Dull Weather, 1880
Oil on canvas, 68 x 90 cm
*Calouste Gulbenkian Foundation,
Lisbon*

215 • The Frost, 1880
Oil on canvas, 61 x 100 cm
Musée d'Orsay, Paris

**216 • The Thaw on the Seine :
Blocks of Ice, 1880**
Oil on canvas, 60 x 100 cm
Musée d'Orsay, Paris

217 • The Ice Floes, 1880
Oil on canvas, 97 x 150 cm
*Shelburne Museum, Shelburne
(Vermont)*

**218 • The Thaw on the Seine
at Vetheuil, 1880**
Oil on canvas, 60 x 100 cm
Private Collection

219 • The Thaw, 1880
Oil on canvas, 61 x 100 cm
Hoffmann Collection

220 • Sunflowers, 1880
Oil on canvas, 101 x 81 cm
*The Metropolitan Museum of Art,
New York*

221 • Springtime, 1880
Oil on canvas, 60 x 81 cm
Musée des Beaux-Arts, Lyon

222 • Chrysanthemums, 1880
Oil on canvas, 100 x 81 cm
*The Metropolitan Museum of Art,
New York*

213   214

215   216

217   218

219

220   221   222

223

224

225

226

227

228

229

230

231

232

223 • Bouquet of Hollyhocks, 1880
Oil on canvas, 100 x81 cm
Courtauld Institute Galleries, London

224 • Asters, 1880
Oil on canvas, 83 x 68 cm
Wallis Collection, Los Angeles

225 • Red Chrysanthemums, 1880
Oil on canvas, 82 x 65 cm
Private Collection

226 • The Thaw Near Vétheuil, 1880
Oil on canvas, 65 x 93 cm
Musée du Louvre, Paris

227 • The Thaw, 1880
Oil on canvas, 72 x 100 cm
Musée des Beaux-Arts, Lille

228 • Lavacourt, 1880
Oil on canvas, 100 x 150 cm
Museum of Fine Arts, Dallas

**229 • Sunset on the Seine,
Winter Effect, 1880**
Oil on canvas, 100 x 152 cm
Musée du Petit Palais, Paris

**230 • View of Vétheuil, Thaw,
1880 (?)**
Oil on canvas, 71 x 100 cm
Private Collection

231 • Town of Vétheuil, 1881
Oil on canvas, 14 x 22 cm
Musée des Beaux-Arts, Rouen

232 • Hillside Near Vétheuil, 1881
Oil on canvas, 14 x 22 cm
Musée des Beaux-Arts, Rouen

WORKS

233 • The Seine from the Heights of Chantemesle, 1881
Oil on canvas, 14 x 22 cm
Musée des Beaux-Arts, Rouen

234 • The Artist's Garden at Vétheuil, 1881
Oil on canvas, 150 x 120 cm
National Gallery of Art, Washington

235 • Portrait of Monsieur Coqueret (Son), 1881
Oil on canvas, 46 x 38 cm
The Art Institute, Chicago

236 • The Sea Seen from the Cliff, 1881
Oil on canvas, 60 x 75 cm
Private Collection

237 • Calm Weather, Fécamp, 1881
Oil on canvas, 60 x 73.5 cm
Rudolf Staechelin Foundation, Basel

238 • The Seine at Vétheuil, 1881
Oil on canvas, 66 x 81 cm
Private Collection

239 • Woman Seated in a Garden, 1881
Oil on canvas, 81 x 65 cm
Private Collection

240 • The Coast at Trouville, 1881
Oil on canvas, 60 x 81 cm
Museum of Fine Arts, Boston

241 • Stranded Ship, 1881
Oil on canvas, 80 x 60 cm
Private Collection

242 • The Sea at Fécamp, 1881
Oil on canvas, 65 x 82 cm
Staatsgalerie, Stuttgart

233

234

235

236

237

238

239

240

241

242

243

244

245

246

247

248

249

250

251

252

243 • The Cliff Near Dieppe, 1882
Oil on canvas, 65 x 81 cm
Kunsthaus, Zurich

**244 • The Cliff-Walk
at Pourville, 1882**
Oil on canvas, 65 x 81 cm
Nationalmuseum, Stockholm

**245 • The Cliff-Walk,
Pourville, 1882**
Oil on canvas, 65 x 81 cm
The Art Institute, Chicago

**246 • The Cliff-Walk
at Pourville, 1882**
Oil on canvas, 60 x 81 cm
*The Metropolitan Museum of Art,
New York*

247 • Low Tide at Pourville, 1882
Oil on canvas, 60 x 81 cm
The Museum of Art, Cleveland

**248 • At Dusk with Mist
at Pourville, 1882**
Oil on canvas, 60 x 73 cm
*Maxwell-Cummings Collection,
Canada*

249 • A Park in Pourville, 1882
Oil on canvas, 65 x 81 cm
Private Collection

**250 • Fishing Area
at Pourville, 1882**
Oil on canvas, 60 x 81 cm
Haags Gemeentemuseum, The Hague

251 • Madame Paul (Mère Paul), 1882
Oil on canvas, 65 x 54 cm
*The Fogg Art Museum, Cambridge
(Massachusetts)*

252 • Monsieur Paul (Père Paul), 1882
Oil on canvas, 64 x 51 cm
Kunsthistorisches Museum, Vienna

WORKS

253 • The Cakes, 1882
Oil on canvas, 65 x 81 cm
Private Collection

254 • Low Tide at Pourville, 1882
Oil on canvas, 60 x 81 cm
*Maxwell-Cummings Collection,
Canada*

255 • The Gorge at Varengeville, 1882
Oil on canvas, 65 x 81 cm
Private Collection

**256 • The Customs-Officers' Cabin,
Varengeville, 1882**
Oil on canvas, 60 x 78 cm
*Museum Boymans-van Beuningen,
Rotterdam*

**257 • The Customs-Officers' Cabin,
Dieppe, 1882**
Oil on canvas, 58.4 x 69.8 cm
*The Metropolitan Museum of Art,
New York*

**258 • Fishermen's House at
Varengeville, 1882**
Oil on canvas, 61 x 88 cm
Museum of Fine Arts, Boston

**259 • The Customs-Officers'
Cabin, 1882**
Oil on canvas, 60 x 81 cm
The Museum of Art, Philadelphia

**260 • The Church at Varengeville,
Morning Effect, 1882**
Oil on canvas, 60 x 73 cm
Museum of Fine Arts, Houston

**261 • The Church at Varengeville,
Morning Effect, 1882**
Oil on canvas, 60 x 73 cm
Private Collection

**262 • The Church at Varengeville,
Sunset, 1882**
Oil on canvas, 65 x 81 cm
Private Collection

253

254

255

256

257

258

259

260

261

262

263

264

265

266

267

268

269

270

271

272

263 • Line Fishermen on the Seine Near Poissy, 1882
Oil on canvas, 60 x 82 cm
Kunsthistorisches Museum, Vienna

264 • Low Tide at Pourville, Misty Weather, 1882
Oil on canvas, 60 x 81 cm
Lloyd-Kreeger Collection

265 • Cliffs Near Pourville, 1882
Oil on canvas, 60 x 81 cm
Enschede Collection

266 • Christmas Roses, 1883
Oil on canvas, 50 x 37 cm
Private Collection

267 • Étretat : The Beach and the Port of Amont, 1883
Oil on canvas, 66 x 81 cm
Musée d'Orsay, Paris

268 • Turbulent Sea, Étretat, 1883
Oil on canvas, 81 x 100 cm
Musée des Beaux-Arts, Lyon

269 • Morning at Étretat, 1883
Oil on canvas, 65 x 81 cm
The Art Institute, Chicago

270 • The Rock Arch at Étretat (The Manneporte), 1883
Oil on canvas, 65.4 x 81.3 cm
The Metropolitan Museum of Art, New York

271 • The Manneporte Seen from Below, 1883
Oil on canvas, 73 x 92 cm
Private Collection

272 • The Small Islands of Port-Villez, 1883
Oil on canvas, 65 x 92 cm
Private Collection

WORKS

273 • Landscape at Villez Near Vernon, 1883
Oil on canvas, 73 x 32 cm
Private Collection

274 • Michel Monet with Blue Sweater, 1883
Oil on canvas, 46 x 38 cm
Musée Marmottan, Paris

275 • The Seine at Port-Villez, 1883
Oil on canvas, 60 x 100 cm
Acquavella Galleries

276 • Palm Trees at Bordighera, 1884
Oil on canvas, 65 x 81 cm
The Metropolitan Museum of Art, New York

277 • The Sasso Valley, Sun Light Effect, 1884
Oil on canvas, 65 x 81 cm
Musée Marmottan, Paris

278 • Valle Buona, 1884
Oil on canvas, 65 x 92 cm
Private Collection

279 • View of Bordighera, 1884
Oil on canvas, 65 x 81 cm
A. Hammer Collection, Los Angeles

280 • Bordighera, 1884
Oil on canvas, 65 x 81 cm
The Art Institute, Chicago

281 • Study of Olive Trees, Bordighera, 1884
Oil on canvas, 60 x 73 cm
Private Collection

282 • Under the Lemon Trees, 1884
Oil on canvas, 73 x 60 cm
Ny Carlsberg Glyptotek, Copenhagen

273

274

275

276

277

278

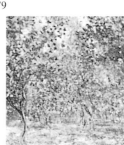
279

280

281

282

283   284

285   286

287   288

289   290

291   292

283 • The Castle of Dolce Acqua, 1884
Oil on canvas, 92 x 73 cm
Musée Marmottan, Paris

284 • The Castle of Dolce Acqua, 1884
Oil on canvas, 73 x 92 cm
Private Collection

285 • The Valley of Nervia, 1884
Oil on canvas, 65 x 81 cm
The Metropolitan Museum of Art, New York

286 • View from Vintimille, 1884
Oil on canvas, 65 x 81 cm
Private Collection

287 • Menton, Landscape Seen from Cape Martin, 1884
Oil on canvas, 68 x 83 cm
Museum of Fine Arts, Boston

288 • Reddish Landscape Near Menton, 1884
Oil on canvas, 65 x 81 cm
The Art Institute, Chicago

289 • Branch of an Orange Tree, 1884
Oil on canvas, 50 x 37 cm
Private Collection

290 • The Cliffs of Aval with the Arch and the Needle, 1884
Oil on canvas, 60 x 81 cm
Kunstmuseum, Basel

291 • Stacks of Wheat, Evening Effect, 1884
Oil on canvas, 65 x 81 cm
Pushkin Museum, Moscow

292 • The Beach and the Cliffs of Aval at Étretat, 1884
Oil on canvas, 60 x 73 cm
Samuel Dorsky Collection

WORKS

293 • Three Fishing Boats, 1885
Oil on canvas, 73 x 92 cm
Magyar Nemzeti Múzeum, Budapest

294 • Anemones, 1885
Oil on canvas, 50 x 37 cm
Private Collection

295 • The Cliffs and the Port of Amont; Morning Effect, 1885
Oil on canvas, 50 x 61 cm
Musée Marmottan, Paris

296 • The Needle and the Cliffs at Aval, 1885
Oil on canvas, 65 x 81 cm
Sterling and Francine Clark Art Institute, Williamstown

297 • Poppy Field in a Hollow Near Giverny, 1885
Oil on canvas, 65 x 81 cm
Museum of Fine Arts, Boston

298 • Fishing Boats on the Beach, Étretat, 1885
Oil on canvas, 65 x 81 cm
The Art Institute, Chicago

299 • The Manneporte, High Tide, 1885
Oil on canvas, 65 x 81 cm
Private Collection

300 • The Stack of Wheat, 1885
Oil on canvas, 61 x 81 cm
The Hermitage Museum, St. Petersburg

301 • The Seine Near Giverny, 1885
Oil on canvas, 65 x 92 cm
Private Collection

302 • Étretat, The Arch of Aval at Étretat: Fishing Boats Leaving the Port, 1885 (?)
Oil on canvas, 60 x 81 cm
Musée des Beaux-Arts, Dijon

293

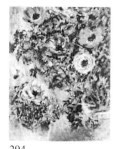
294

295

296

297

298

299

300

301

302

303

304

305

306

307

308

309

310

311

312

303 • Fields of Tulips in Holland, 1886
Oil on canvas, 65 x 81 cm
Musée d'Orsay, Paris

304 • Woman with a Sunshade Turned to the Right: Attempt at Figure Painting Outdoors, 1886
Oil on canvas, 131 x 88 cm
Musée d'Orsay, Paris

305 • Woman with a Sunshade Turned to the Left: Attempt at Figure Painting Outdoors, 1886
Oil on canvas, 131 x 88 cm
Musée d'Orsay, Paris

306 • Self-Portrait, 1886
Oil on canvas, 56 x 46 cm
Private Collection

307 • Departure of Fishing Boats at Étretat, 1886
Oil on canvas, 66 x 81 cm
Pushkin Museum, Moscow

308 • Rain at Étretat, 1886
Oil on canvas, 60 x 73 cm
Nasjonalgalleriet, Oslo

309 • The Manneporte Near Étretat, 1886
Oil on canvas, 81.3 x 65.4 cm
The Metropolitan Museum of Art, New York

310 • The Manneporte, 1886
Oil on canvas, 92 x 73 cm
Private Collection

311 • The Pyramides at Port-Coton, Rough Sea, 1886
Oil on canvas, 65 x 81 cm
Pushkin Museum, Moscow

312 • The Pyramides at Port-Coton, Sun Effect, 1886
Oil on canvas, 64 x 64 cm
Private Collection

WORKS

313 • Storm at Belle-Île, 1886
Oil on canvas, 65 x 81 cm
Musée d'Orsay, Paris

314 • Portrait of Poli, 1886
Oil on canvas, 74 x 53 cm
Musée Marmottan, Paris

315 • The Rocks of Belle-Île, 1886
Oil on canvas, 65 x 81 cm
Musée d'Orsay, Paris

316 • Belle-Île, 1886
Oil on canvas, 60 x 80 cm
Musée Rodin, Paris

317 • Belle-Île. Rain Effect, 1886
Oil on canvas, 60 x 73 cm
Bridgestone Museum of Art, Tokyo

318 • Port-Coton, the Lion, 1886
Oil on canvas, 60 x 73 cm
Private Collection

319 • Storm at Belle-Île, 1886
Oil on canvas, 60 x 73 cm
Private Collection

320 • Rocks at Belle-Île, 1886
Oil on canvas, 66 x 82 cm
Silberman Collection, New York

**321 • Jean-Pierre Hoschedé
and Michel Monet on the Banks
of the Epte, 1887**
Oil on canvas, 76 x 97 cm
Bronfman Collection, Montreal

**322 • Blanche Hoschedé Painting and
Suzanne Hoschedé Reading, 1887**
Oil on canvas, 91 x 98 cm
Formerly Alex Maguy Collection

313

314

315

316

317

318

319

320

321

322

323

324

325

326

327

328

329

330

331

332

323 • White Clematis, 1887
Oil on canvas, 92 x 52 cm
Musée Marmottan, Paris

324 • Clematis, 1887
Oil on canvas, 65 x 10 cm
Private Collection

325 • Peonies, 1887
Oil on canvas, 65 x 100 cm
National Museum of Western Art,
Tokyo

326 • Under the Poplars,
Sunlight Effect, 1887
Oil on canvas, 74 x 93 cm
Staatsgalerie, Stuttgart

327 • Boating on the Epte, 1887
Oil on canvas, 133 x 145 cm
Museu de Arte, São Paulo

328 • The Blue Boat, 1887
Oil on canvas, 109 x 129 cm
Private Collection

329 • Young Girls in a Boat, 1887
Oil on canvas, 145 x 132 cm
National Museum of Western Art,
Tokyo

330 • In the Norvégienne, 1887
Oil on canvas, 98 x 131 cm
Musée d'Orsay, Paris

331 • The Empty Boat, 1887
Oil on canvas, 146 x 133 cm
Musée Marmottan, Paris

332 • Poplars at Giverny, 1887
Oil on canvas, 73 x 92 cm
The Museum of Modern Art, New York

WORKS

333 • Antibes, Evening Effects, 1888
Oil on canvas, 66 x 81 cm
Museum of Fine Arts, Boston

**334 • Gardener's House
at Antibes, 1888**
Oil on canvas, 65 x 92 cm
The Museum of Art, Cleveland

335 • Antibes Seen from La Salis, 1888
Oil on canvas, 73 x 92 cm
Museum of Art, Toledo (Ohio)

336 • The Mountains of Esterel, 1888
Oil on canvas, 65 x 92 cm
Courtauld Institute Galleries, London

337 • The Mediterranean, 1888
Oil on canvas, 60 x 73 cm
Private Collection

338 • The Sea at Antibes, 1888
Oil on canvas, 65 x 81 cm
Museum der Stadt, Wuppertal

**339 • Pine Trees,
the Cape of Antibes, 1888**
Oil on canvas, 73 x 92 cm
Private Collection

**340 • Angels Bay, from the Cape
of Antibes, 1888**
Oil on canvas, 65 x 81 cm
Rosensaft Collection

341 • Meadows at Giverny, 1888
Oil on canvas, 92 x 80 cm
*The Hermitage Museum,
St. Petersburg*

342 Antibes Bay, 1888
Oil on canvas, 65 x 92 cm
Private Collection

333

334

335

336

337

338

339

341

342

343

344

345

346

347

348

349

350

351

352

343 • The Bridge at Vervy, 1889
Oil on canvas, 65 x 92 cm
Musée Marmottan, Paris

**344 • The Creuse Ravine
at Twilight, 1889**
Oil on canvas, 65 x 81 cm
Musée des Beaux-Arts, Reims

**345 • The «Petite Creuse» Rapids
at Fresselines, 1889**
Oil on canvas, 65 x 92 cm
*The Metropolitan Museum of Art,
New York*

346 • The Rock, 1889
Oil on canvas, 73 x 92 cm
Royal Collections, Great Britain

**347 • Sunset in the
Creuse Valley, 1889**
Oil on canvas, 73 x 70 cm
Musée d'Unterlinden, Colmar

348 • The Seine at Port-Villez, 1890
Oil on canvas, 65 x 92 cm
Musée d'Orsay, Paris

349 • Poppy Field, 1890
Oil on canvas, 60 x 92 cm
*The Hermitage Museum, St.
Petersburg*

**350 • Stacks of Wheat, Late
Summer: Morning Effect, 1890**
Oil on canvas, 60.5 x 100.5 cm
Musée d'Orsay, Paris

351 • Field of Oats with Poppies, 1890
Oil on canvas, 65 x 92 cm
Musée d'Art moderne, Strasbourg

352 • Poplars on the Epte, 1891
Oil on canvas, 92 x 73 cm
The Tate Gallery, London

WORKS

353 • Poplars on the Epte, 1891
Oil on canvas, 80 x 92 cm
Private Collection

**354 • Rouen Cathedral, the Portal
Seen from the Front, Harmony
in Brown, 1892**
Oil on canvas, 107 x 73 cm
Musée d'Orsay, Paris

**355 • Rouen Cathedral, Front door,
Dull Weather, 1892**
Oil on canvas, 100 x 65 cm
Musée d'Orsay, Paris

**356 • Rouen Cathedral, the Portal
and the Tour Saint-Romain,
Morning Effect, Harmony
in White, 1893**
Oil on canvas, 106 x 73 cm
Musée d'Orsay, Paris

**357 • Rouen Cathedral,
the West Portal and the Tour
d'Albane, Blue Harmony, 1893**
Oil on canvas, 91 x 63 cm
Musée d'Orsay, Paris

**358 • Rouen Cathedral, the West
Portal and the Tour d'Albane,
Full Sunlight, 1893**
Oil on canvas, 107 x 73 cm
Musée d'Orsay, Paris

**359 • Rouen Cathedral,
the Portal, 1893**
Oil on canvas, 100 x 65 cm
National Gallery of Art, Washington

**360 • Norwegian Landscape,
Blue Houses, 1895**
Oil on canvas, 61 x 84 cm
Musée Marmottan, Paris

361 • Mount Kolsaas at Norway, 1895
Oil on canvas, 65.5 x 100 cm
Musée d'Orsay, Paris

362 • Cape of Antibes, 1896
Oil on canvas, 73 x 92 cm
The National Gallery, London

353

354

355

356

357

358

359

360

361

362

363

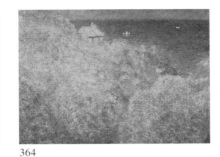

364

365

366

367

368

369

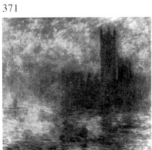

370

371

372

363 • The Seine at Giverny, 1897
Oil on canvas, 81 x 100 cm
National Gallery of Art, Washington

**364 • Cliffs at Varengeville
(The Petit-Ailly Gorge), 1897**
Oil on canvas, 65 x 92 cm
Musée des Beaux-Arts, Le Havre

**365 • Branch of the Seine Near
Giverny, 1897**
Oil on canvas, 75 x 92.5 cm
Musée d'Orsay, Paris

**366 • The Water Lily Pool,
Harmony in Green, 1899**
Oil on canvas, 89 x 93.5 cm
Musée d'Orsay, Paris

**367 • The Water Lily Pool,
Harmony in Rose, 1900**
Oil on canvas, 89.5 x 100 cm
Musée d'Orsay, Paris

**368 • The Artist's Garden
in Giverny, 1900**
Oil on canvas, 81 x 92 cm
Musée d'Orsay, Paris

**369 • Morning at Vétheuil,
1900 or 1901**
Oil on canvas, 89 x 92 cm
Musée des Beaux-Arts, Lille

**370 • Vétheuil, at Sunset,
1900 or 1901**
Oil on canvas, 89 x 92 cm
Musée d'Orsay, Paris

**371 • Waterloo Bridge,
Effect of Sunlight, 1903**
Oil on canvas, 64 x 100 cm
Carnegie Museum of Art, Pittsburgh

**372 • London, Houses of Parliament,
Westminster Towers, 1903**
Oil on canvas, 81 x 92 cm
Musée des Beaux-Arts, Le Havre

WORKS

**373 • Houses of Parliament,
Sun Shining through the Fog, 1904**
Oil on canvas, 81 x 92 cm
Musée d'Orsay, Paris

**374 • Houses of Parliament,
Stormy Weather, 1904**
Oil on canvas, 81 x 92 cm
Musée des Beaux-Arts, Lille

375 • Water Lily Pond, 1904
Oil on canvas, 90 x 92 cm
Musée des Beaux-Arts, Caen

376 • Water Lilies, 1904
Oil on canvas, 90 x 93 cm
Musée des Beaux-Arts, Le Havre

377 • Water Lilies, 1907
Oil on canvas, 80 cm
*Musée d'Art et d'Industrie,
Saint-Étienne*

378 • The Da Mula Palace, 1908
Oil on canvas, 62 x 81 cm
National Gallery of Art, Washington

**379 • Venice, The Ducal Palace Seen
from San Giorgio Maggiore, 1908**
Oil on canvas, 65 x 100 cm
Private Collection

380 • Gondolas at Venice, 1908
Oil on canvas, 81 x 55 cm
Musée des Beaux-Arts, Nantes

381 • Water Lilies, 1908
Oil on canvas, 90 cm
*Musée Alphonse-Georges Poulin,
Vernon*

382 • Water Lilies, Sunset Effect, 1910
Oil on canvas, 202 x 630 cm
Kunsthaus, Zurich

373

374

375

376

377

378

379

380

381

382

383

384

385

386

387

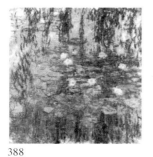

388

389

390

391

383 • The Clouds, 1914-1918
Oil on canvas
(three panels), 197 x 1271 cm
Musée de l'Orangerie, Paris

**384 • Water Lilies: Morning,
1914-1918**
Oil on canvas
(three panels), 197 x 1211 cm
Musée de l'Orangerie, Paris

385 • Green Reflections, 1914-1918
Oil on canvas
(two panels), 197 x 847 cm
Musée de l'Orangerie, Paris

386 • Sunset, 1914-1918
Oil on canvas, 197 x 594 cm
Musée de l'Orangerie, Paris

387 • Self-Portrait, 1917
Oil on canvas, 70 x 55 cm
Musée de l'Orangerie, Paris

388 • Blue Water Lilies, 1916-1919
Oil on canvas, 200 x 200 cm
Musée d'Orsay, Paris

389 • Water Lilies at Giverny, 1917
Oil on canvas, 100 x 200 cm
Musée des Beaux-Arts, Nantes

390 • Yellow Iris
Oil on canvas, 150 x 130 cm
Formerly E. Tériade Collection

391 • Wisteria
Oil on canvas, 100 x 200 cm
*Musée d'Art et d'Histoire Marcel-
Dessal, Dreux*

Bibliography

Hommage à Monet, catalogue of the Exhibition, Galeries nationales du Grand Palais, Paris, 1980

J. ISAACSON, *Claude Monet, observation et réflexion,* Neufchâtel, 1978

CH.S. MOFFET, *The New Painting. Impressionism 1874-1876,* catalogue of the Exhibition, Fine Arts Museum of San Francisco; National Gallery of Art, Washington, 1986

Monet in the 90s, The Series Paintings, catalogue of the Exhibition, Museum of Fine Arts, Boston; Art Institute, Chicago; Royal Academy of Arts, London, 1990

S. MONNERET, *Dictionnaire de l'Impressionnisme et son époque,* Paris, 1978 ("Collection Bouquins", 1987)

S. PATIN, *Monet "Un œil...mais bon Dieu, quel œil !",* (Découvertes Gallimard), Paris,1991

J. REWALD, *The History of Impressionism,* New York, 1946

L. ROSSI BORTOLATTO, *Tout l'œuvre peint de Monet 1870-1889,* Paris, 1981

V. SPATE, *Claude Monet. Time of colours,* London, 1992

CH. F. STUCKEY, *Monet, A Retrospective,* New York, 1985

P.H. TUCKER, *Monet at Argenteuil,* New Haven-London, 1982

D. WILDENSTEIN, *Claude Monet, biographie et catalogue raisonné,* Lausanne-Paris, 1974-1985

Picture Credits

Agence photographique de la Réunion des Musées Nationaux, RMN, Paris
76, 77

AISA, Archivo Iconográfico, S.A. , Barcelona
6, 9, 24, 25, 26, 27, 28, 29, 30, 31, 34, 35, 36, 37, 40, 41, 44, 45, 46, 47, 48, 49, 50, 51, 52, 53, 54, 55, 60, 61, 62, 63, 64, 65, 66, 67, 68, 69, 70, 71, 72, 73, 74, 75, 78,79, 80, 81, 82, 83

Bibliothèque Nationale de France, Paris
4, 11, 15, 17

Museum of Fine Arts, Boston
58, 59

National Gallery of Art, Washington, D.C.
56, 57

Roger-Viollet, Parijs
5, 7, 8, 10, 13, 14, 16, 19, 20, 21, 23

The Metropolitan Museum of Art, New York
32, 33, 38, 39

The Walters Art Gallery, Baltimore
42, 43

The publisher wishes to express gratitude to the photographer, Alfredo Dagli Orti, for his valuable collaboration.